Mainly Sentimental

Left to right:
Top row:

| Duncan MacCallum (oilskin) and friend on HMS Vidette 1943 | Sarah Miller McGhie 1906 | Big Ben, London 1966 |

Middle row:

| Sarah MacCallum (née McGhie) 1967 | Lion's Gate Bridge, Vancouver 1996 |

Bottom row:

| St Abbs, Berwickshire, 1996 | Tennis party, St Abbs, 1930 |

＊❤＊

MAINLY

SENTIMENTAL

Poems of a Lifetime

by

Colin MacCallum, PEng

Colin MacCallum (signature)

Erotic, Straight, or Sentimental

Erotic, straight, or sentimental?
Sounds rather rude, you'll say!
　　Depends on your mood,
　　Depends on the food,
Depends on the music they play.

Now, I don't know what you thought I meant!
　　It's poems I'm meaning, you see!
　　Some inane, and some profane,
　　Poems of May, or June - or Jane,
Which I hope you'll share with me!

＊❤＊

✳❤✳

First published 1996
First impression: 950 paperback; 50 hardcover

Published by
MacCallum Boiler Associates
Shingle Spit 1-1
4130 Parnell Road
Hornby Island, BC
V0R 1Z0
Canada

Published with no financial assistance whatsoever from the taxpayer.

Photographs by Jim MacCallum, Vancouver, and Bob Cain, Hornby Island, as indicated. Other photos are family photos.

Cover layout concept by Colin and Jane MacCallum;
  finalized by Steve Penner.

Printed and bound in Canada by Friesens Corporation.

Canadian Cataloguing in Publication Data

Main Entry under title:
  Mainly Sentimental

  ISBN 1-55056-427-7

1.   Canadian poetry (English) - 20th century.
1.   MacCallum, C., 1935-

✳❤✳

INTRODUCTION

It was 1975 and the last hour of the last session of a Technical Writing course with Sandwell professional engineers. As instructor, the present writer gave the final assignment, a choice of writing topics, and added a further challenging one, "The Engineer and the Architect". Imagine her delighted surprise when one participant handed in not only "The Engineer and the Architect" in eight four-line stanzas but also a fistful of limericks.

That participant was Colin MacCallum. This volume has forty years of versifying in its varying moods - joyful, rueful, humourous, serious, nostalgic, evaluating, fanticizing, realistic, sensitive, caustic, accepting, critical. For Mr MacCallum is a man of wide interests. Consider the subjects that encompass his zestful response to all that makes up life: childhood, homeland, family, friends, community, country, universe, nature, love, death, time. His multiplicity of themes indicates richness of personality, joyous commitment to life, and above all, sense of values.

As he writes:

> The words come rolling down the glen -
> It only happens now and then,
> But when it does, I tell ye
> I have to write them!

This volume of verse is a beguiling record of the years.

A.F. Livesey

❤

Colin MacCallum in December 1995

✳❤✳

FOREWORD

These poems have been written over a period of about forty years - since I was about eighteen.

The poems are about the loves, and life, of a sentimental man, a Glasgow-born Scot, mechanical engineer - a specialist in the design of large boilers for pulp mills and power stations - enthusiastic, optimistic and with a reputation for being well-versed in his field and for calling a spade a spade. All my poems, to date, appear on these pages, except for three or four love poems to my wife, Jane.

The poems are dated and presented in chronological order, from the age of sixty, back into the past. I hope you enjoy reading them as much as I have enjoyed writing them!

Acknowledgements

My many thanks for ongoing encouragement are due to my wife, Jane and to the rest of my family and friends who have been supportive over the years. Jack Forster, my friend and colleague in West Vancouver, Bill Yeomans and the late Ted Walker, on Hornby Island, have always been particularly supportive.

I also must thank Adelia Livesey, not just for her comments on style, but for reminding me of the fine line between fun and vulgarity!

My brother Jim in Vancouver, took most of the photographs, other than one or two older family photos. The photographs of Hornby Island were provided by Bob Cain.

The poem "London" will be published in "This England's Country Calendar 1997".

Colin MacCallum
Hornby Island
March 1996

❋❤❋

❋❤❋

To Jane

❤

Contents

✳❤✳

＊♥＊

❋❤❋

❋❤❋

❋❤❋

Letters From A Destroyer - HMS Vidette

These letters from a bygone age,
When Hitler's war was all the rage
And men like Churchill held the stage
    Seem bland, but then
A careless word would just enrage
    The censor's pen.

"We had a quiet crossing, Dear"
Are words he knows she wants to hear
And "Halifax" is "over here";
    All well-intentioned;
The U-boat menace, ever near,
    Is never mentioned.

At Omaha, in D-Day's glow,
Dad writes "When things were rather slow
We sat on deck and watched the show" -
    with senses sated;
He doesn't write that, down below,
    A death-trap waited.

En route from leave, a waiting room,
He writes of Love, that blushing bloom,
While anti-aircraft cannons boom
    At terrors horrid;
A recent love we must assume
    Was often torrid.

      Hornby Island
      1996.02.21

Castle Rock and Jock's Nose, St Abbs

The Rose

The east wind rips the spume from the waves
and the words from your mouth as well!
A trough in the crests shows the blackened tooth
of the Ebb Carr - straight from Hell!
The waves pound in to the rocky shore,
you can feel their crashing shock
As the spray obscures Jock's Nose and flies
to the height of the Castle Rock.

The crests roll in to the harbour wall
in a foaming, seething mass;
The spindrift flies up the steep hillside
and sticks to the tortured grass;
You can hardly stand on the cliffside path
or see for the driving snow,
But you hear the roar of the pounding surf
on the rugged rocks, below.

The waves dash and foam in to Coldingham Sands
and the wind funnels in to the shore
And up to the daunting Priory walls,
there, seven hundred years and more,
Buffets an elegant archway ruin
and sinks with a sighing moan
And rustles the leaves on a new little rose
by a peaceful granite stone.

Hornby Island, 1996.02.04

✳❤✳

It's Nice to Know

It's nice to know the world will turn,
The rain will fall, the rivers run;
It's nice to know that every spring
The leaves will bud, the birds will sing,
Even when I'm gone.

It's nice to know that children's charms
Will gladden mothers' loving arms,
Even when I'm gone.

It's nice to know that Love's sweet tune
Will still be sung beneath the moon;
That sparkling, youthful eyes will shine
With young love's sweetness, arms entwine,
As lovers stroll on shady paths,
All hawthorn-scented, luscious grass,
In lilac time,
Even when I'm gone.

I'd like to take some bad with me -
A withered twig of family tree;
But perhaps some good will stay -
My private piece of earthly clay
To fertilize a rose one day,
To blossom when I'm gone.

But, 'til then I'll live each minute,
Love the world and all that's in it,
Love it till I'm gone.

Fish Hoek
1996.01.14

♥

Happy Holidays

The days till I'm home drift so slowly away,
The calendar's dragging its feet.
These days in the sunshine are interesting, true,
- But I'd rather be home with my sweet!

The wind's strong and ceaseless, the waves towering, blue,
The sand is like flour 'neath my feet;
But swimming alone really isn't much fun,
- I'd much rather bathe with my sweet!

The wind rushes on, but the clock 's stuck at four -
Another night far from complete;
No one to talk to and no one to hug;
- Another night far from my sweet!

I've read, I've swum, sent postcards home and also a long letter,
But best of all, I've got to know my aunt and cousin better.

In the small hours of the morn,
When each second is a thorn,
One long interminable groan
To be on holiday - alone!

Fish Hoek
1996.01.13

The Visitor

I waken - hear the wind, the crashing sea;
The curtains dance and flutter by the bed;
Faint skeins of dreams, all tangled in my head;
And, all cosy, curled in comfort there -
A little tabby cat, asleep upon my chair.

She stirs, she smiles, she scratches, curls around -
A wraith who comes and goes without a sound.

Fish Hoek
1996.01.13

＊♥＊

Near Miss in Cape Town

I leave the station, cross the busy street,
Pass the hawkers, selling beads and baubles
Strewn on blankets by their feet.

I gaze and linger, then become aware,
A strange and violent feeling hanging in the air
- The glance, the look, the quick-averted stare.

I cross again - from shadow into sun;
The feeling disappears as fast as it's begun.

Handsome buildings, dappled trees,
Coloured dresses, coal-black children, sunburned knees.

Retrace my path - the tension's there again -
An animal intensity - like pain -
Gnawing, stabbing.

An escalator? No - I use the stair,
Uneasy and aware, as I descend,
I see two men have reached the other end
And turn and ask me - Do I have the time?
No - then I brush past as I decline.
The subway's short and many people there.
Out again, breathe again, in the open air.

Suddenly a powerful, thrusting, grabbing!
I grasp the thrusting hand;
Petrified we stand.
I swear, I twist and suddenly we fall.
I twist away and scramble to the wall.

Assailants flee, still unseen -
Strangers stare - am I unclean?
Wallet safe. Quite out of breath.
Not a bruise - lovely life -
Lucky break - no club or knife!
Nearly a statistic - unnecessary death.

Fish Hoek
1996.01.12

Anticipation - Sweet?

I face each trip with trepidation
Think of the dangers I might meet,
Perhaps a chance assassination
- The fall from forty thousand feet!

No matter what my destination
my travel plans are incomplete;
Does Heaven await - or dark damnation -
A bomb in a bin on a distant street?

Should I subscribe to predestination?
Is there a shark in the sea not yet replete,
Cruising to a meeting off Cape Town station
To a meal of an arm or both my feet?

I hope this awareness of my life's fragility
Is not just a sign of advancing senility!

Hornby Island
1995.12.28

Note:

(This poetic premonition, just a simple superstition,
Very nearly came to pass - in a Cape Town underpass -
Somewhat south of the Equator,
Can you believe it, two weeks later!!)

Natural Selection

I understand that docs and vets
Are just as skilled and tutored -
But the vet's the man to go and see
If you're just wanting neutered!

Hornby Island
1995.12.27

❄❤❄

Topsy-turvey Realization

I saw a bald young chap today
Whose beard was long and brown -
When suddenly I realized
His head was upside down!

Hornby Island
1995.12.25

The Immigrant

A little boy once came to stay,
Small and fair and rather glum;
Brother Peter, little sister,
Doctor Dad and bustling Mum.

He seldom mingled with the others,
Hard to please in many ways;
He'd read a book, or sit there quietly,
Met the world with troubled gaze.

Bursts of brightness, then withdrawn;
At breakfast he seemed simply thrawn!
Would he like ham, or eggs, or porridge,
Oatcake, jam, or Scottish brose?
But, at each renewed suggestion
He'd wrinkle up his button nose!

Look back - it wasn't easy for that little man -
Sitting there, that little soul -
His world had changed, beyond control.
He missed his chums, his house, his garden -
But most, he missed his loving Gran.

Hornby Island
1995.12.24

✼❤✼

Seize the Golden Moment

Seize the golden moment
and scribble down that line -
Or memory will fail you -
It won't be there next time!

Seize the golden moment
and watch a harvest moon;
Dally with your lover,
The morning comes too soon.

Seize the golden moment,
Savour Childhood's bliss,
Revel in its laughter,
Treasure every kiss.

Chatting in the darkness,
With dawning comes the day,
Seize the golden moment
And kiss the night away!

Prince George
1995.11.30

Ménage a Trois

Bartok was a character, a handsome ginger tom,
Even as a kitten he was boss;
At eight weeks old, a ball of fur and tail up in the air.
Sophie was completely at a loss!

Sophie then was two years old, black with four white paws,
Furry, somewhat timid, lovely eyes;
Twiggy, Burmese, thin and grey, was six months older still.
Bartok simply took them by surprise!
He'd lie in wait and ambush them, from table or from chair;
He'd leap on Sophie, quickly, like a hawk,
But Twiggy, much more fragile, was thirteen times more agile
And escaped from him, grey lightning, with a squawk!

✳❤✳

Bartok liked to lie and snooze upon a bookcase there,
Ginger head upon a snowy paw,
But, as you passed, he'd stretch a leg and smile a friendly smile,
Seeking your attention with a claw.

In course of time we sold the house, and Twiggy ran away.
Sadly, we could only keep one cat -
Alberta friends took Bartok then and made him feel at home
- Our neighbours' cats were really pleased at that!

Sophie's still as timid and she mainly sleeps at home
Dreaming of the way they met their ends,
But Bartok - I can see him eating catfood up in heaven
Surrounded by his nubile female friends!

Prince George
1995.11.29

Tantrum at the Opera

In the bar, at intermission,
(The singing had been very good!)
We sipped some champers, most refreshing,
Ordered up a little food.

But when the waiter brought me *gnocchi*
First I kneed him in the crotchee,
Then I flung him off the jetty
For forgetting my *spaghetti*!

(Clearly just a made-up story -
Everything was hunky-dory -
Everybody knows that *gnocchi*
Actually rhymes with "rocky"!)

Hornby Island, 1995.11.08

❋♥❋

Summer - Once Upon a Time

I tightly clench my hand, my left,
And suddenly the warp and weft
Of Time slip free.

I tumble through the glass of Time
And, in a garden, hear the chime
- A clock strikes three.
A clock that's in my Grandma's room
Where dust motes sparkle in the gloom
And dazzle me -
A child of four.

Then, by a quiet and shady bower
Where flowering rhododendrons tower,
I grasp a rusty rail and gaze
Across a meadow. Summer haze
Is what I see -
Not the days that were before
Or the years that lie beyond.

My mother's soft and wavy hair
Is dark and clearly outlined there
Against the lilacs by her chair.
I turn my head and see the flare
Of lilies by a pond.

From scented roses, petals fall
And tiny pebbles on the wall
Are sharp in focus, too.

I hear my little brother call -
He's just turned two:
"The told tap tan't turn!" says he
To Gran, who laughs and turns to me
And takes my hand.

All this and more, cascading back,
When I clench my hand.

Colin and Jim
The Schoolhouse
Greenlaw, 1939

Fiumicino
1995.11.04

❤

Dreaming Again

How can it be just half-past-three -
I've been asleep for hours?
I dreamt of cars in Glasgow
And I think I dreamt of flowers;
Of Alan McDonald - a lad I knew in school -
Some sort of motor accident -
An ancient swimming pool.

You were in the water,
I was climbing to the dale,
Clinging very nervously
To a rather flimsy rail.
The platform was quite tiny -
Not much larger than my feet.
"Don't look down - it makes *me* dizzy!"
You called   -   rather sweet!

Two kids then told me where to land -
I could feel them standing there -
So I jumped - and left my stomach
Fifteen metres in the air!

―――――

This was not a premonition
Of an upset-tum condition,
Nor nerves before a swimming rally
- I woke and heard a gondola
Splashing in the alley!

Venice
1995.11.01

✳❤✳

Southern Necropolis, Glasgow

The stillness of this cemetery, derelict and lone,
Short, wet grass and misty air,
Has a sadness all its own.

The yawning portal, bricked up doors
And all the tumbled stones -
A resting place that's more than sad
For what were much-loved bones.

Some young McGees are buried there -
James and Dave McGee,
Another James, just over four,
No tombstone for these three.
Nor yet for Janet, scarce fourteen,
Died 1 November eighteen-seventy-nine -
She would have been a dear great-aunt of mine
- Just paper left, to show she's ever been.

Times were hard and money short
Those many years ago,
But of this graveyard's sorry state
- I'm glad their folks don't know.

                    Venice
                    1995.10.31

✳❤✳

Venetian Vigil

We sat in a square on a red slatted bench
And watched a child at play -
A little girl, huge green balloon,
A rosy square, bright afternoon,
And nothing to do but play!

Two little boys, running here, running there,
Chase pigeons, to and fro.
Such eager feet, excited cries,
Arms outstretched for the pigeon prize,
While afternoon shadows grow.

An old stooping man comes along with his dog.
A part of his daily rounds,
With aimless gait, erratic walk,
While clicking heels and murmured talk
Contribute their gentle sounds.

And an old stone face looks down from his frieze
And longs for the shade of the lacy, green trees.

Venice
1995.10.31

❤

Strange Silence of Venice

The canal thoroughfare
Where motorboats jostle around,
Throatily bubbles - and jars.

Tucked away in a square,
With crowds of people around,
No thunder of buses or cars,
Only pedestrians there.
Not a mechanical sound
- Stranger than being on Mars!

No fumes in the air.
Just clicking of heels on the ground,
The murmur of chatter from bars.

At evening, where
The quietness is simply profound
- The silence of sentinel stars.

Nowhere else can you find, more's the pity,
Silence like this in the midst of a city.

Venice
1995.10.30

✳❤✳

Via Venezia

There's an *al fresco* café in San Marco Square
Where one cup of coffee would pay for the chair!
There's no use complaining, it's written right there
- Eight bucks for each coffee and four for the band!

Out at Murano, the glass is fantastic -
No way you'd mistake it for common old plastic!
A pity the prices are not more elastic
For glass that's reputed the best in the land.

The skyline in mist is a wonderful sight;
Mist that's translucent - an artist's delight
Will hopefully compensate, soon, for that fright
- Eight bucks for the coffee and four for the band!

> I try not to dwell on it,
> But can't sleep well on it!
> Now you've been tipped off
> How we were ripped off -
> Robbed, most unkind,
> By a Venetian, blind,
> In this foreign land!

Venice
1995.10.29

Conundri dell' Italia

Why would a love-lorn lass like Leda[*]
Go for long-necked swans, not dux?
Why do men like splashy sports cars
More than much more macho trux?

Perhaps the answer lies on Lesbos
Where the gals like hens, not cox
And where smooth and silken stockings
Are preferred to ankle sox?

Here are many damaged statues,
Some with crax and some with nix -
Which raises one more towering question -
Who steals all those marble prix?

Florence
1995.10.28

[*] Zeus approached Leda in the form of a swan and fathered the twin,
Pollux, and Helen of Troy, according to Greek legend.

✳❤✳

Impressions of Italy

We've never seen so many simply wondrous works of art,
To late into the evening after morning's shaky start;
We've never seen so many clothes so lavishly displayed,
Colours bright, the fashions right, exciting - nothing staid!

We've walked the streets the Caesars walked,
                              where Leonardo strode;
Wandered, rapt, in palaces, a cobbled roman road;
Touched the head of "Brutus", seen Botticelli's "Spring"
(The maidens so alive you can almost hear them sing!).

The people don't wear baseball hats, runners, scruffy jeans;
No ghetto blasters carried round by crowds of noisy teens.

Oh sure, the traffic noise is bad, the traffic fumes are worse;
The crowds of tourists jostle and the line-ups are a curse,
But people here are friendly folk in spite of all the throngs
Of strangers and the waiters have
                              a lot more rights than wrongs.

If we never saw TV again, we wouldn't miss a thing
If we could be in Italy in autumn or in spring,
Where art is Art, where Culture lives and Elegance is king!

                              Florence
                              1995.10.27

Roman Holiday

Sitting in a sidewalk café, eating antipasto,
Olive oil and bread all crusty,
As the Roman world goes past you,
With your quiet sophistication,
Tailored suit and courtly shoe
And your wine appreciation -
You could be a Roman too!

Domes and cupolas abound,
Cars and scooters hoot around,
Sistine Chapel - scarce a sound.

Gawk, like strangers down the ages;
Off the sidewalk, life at risk;
Wonder-gaze at Trajan's Column
Or a stolen obelisk;

The Pantheon, the Colosseum
And the arches, apostolic.
Late October, cool at eve,
But not a sign of rain or sleet.
Tired of tours, then home to frolic
'Neath a Roman sheet!

Rome
1995.10.20

Kelvingrove in Autumn

Glasgow University,
Cradle of diversity,
Stands above the Kelvin,
With its reading room,
Silent as the tomb,
With books to dig and delve in,
Above far Sauchiehall,
Which is, after all,
Just a long extension
Of a street not worth a mention.

Lovely Kelvingrove,
Where lads and lasses rove
And you know you're getting old
When the grass feels wet and cold!

Glasgow
1995.10.13

St Abbs School Museum

D'ye ken John Craig wi' his smile sae gay?
D'ye ken John Craig now he's hame tae stay?
D'ye ken John Craig wi' his winning way,
  As he swings tae the skule in the morning?

Oh, the sound of his voice still lilts in my head;
He's a grand wee chap and he's quite well read
As he maks his notes o' the quick an' the dead,
  As he works for the skule night and morning.

And we'll no' forget a' the work he's done,
Wi' his old skule pal, Billy An-der-son -
The museum's a success, a success hard won -
  Well worth a visit in the morning.

And if ye should come in the afternoon,
Dinnae jist rush roon', hae a wee sit doon,
But rest assured, if ye leave too soon
  Ye can aye come again in the morning!

     St Abbs
     1995.10.09

❋♥❋

The Road Home to St Abbs
(Where my grandfather was schoolmaster from 1914 to 1933)

On the path from the Heugh in the late afternoon
  there's a saffron-lichened wall
That glows in the rays of the evening sun
  and your shadow is ten feet tall
But you've come from the Head with its towering cliffs
  and you still feel a wee bit small.

Saint Ebba's glance is strange, serene,
  and hints at her awful fate
As she gazes down from her archway there
  where once was a high wood gate
And you hurry past, with quickened pace -
  not just because it's late.

The church tower stands on its emerald mound,
  pure pleasure to the eye;
Raucous rooks are black snowflakes
  in the gleeful gale on high;
Then down past the school, to the old schoolhouse
  and the view where the sea meets sky.

The wind in the wires sings a steady song
  of winters wild and raw,
But tonight on the rim of the darkening sea
  there's a sight that's rare and braw -
The moon coming up, with her red-gold orb -
  the moon my Granddad saw.

St Abbs, 1995.10.08

Sheffield - Silver City

Tradition's mace, its badge, its splendour,
The grandeur of the Cutlers' Hall,
Gleaming plate and candelabra,
The glitter of the annual ball.
    But that's not all!

I hold a goblet, frothily chased,
"From Uncle George" - in 'sixty-three,
A buckle from a bygone era,
A vinaigrette marked "J.M.T.",
A little cup inscribed "To Sarah"
And wonder who the maid might be.

A silver teapot, smooth with years,
A fork, three tines precisely thus,
The craftsman's hands,
    so skilled, yet tender,
Crafting memories, for us.

Sarah Miller McGhie   Sheffield
1907   1995.10.07

Heading North to Scotland

The high road from London goes right past her door.
A detour of inches would open a sore
    and tempt to a tender caress.

If harsh Self-denial is good for the soul
Then I'm heading for Heaven, I guess!

Sheffield
1995.10.07

✳❤✳

Lovely, Lonely, Lady
(To the Queen Mother, In Honour of Her 95th Birthday)

Your Majesty, we see your face
In many a glossy magazine -
It isn't hard to guess
From your carriage and your dress
     You once were Queen.

Your Majesty, we see your hats,
Your smiles, your gloves, your gracious hand,
At durbar, the gymkhana,
From Australia to Ghana,
     Throughout the land.

Your Majesty, we see the smiles
But can't divine the sorrows
Gathered through the years
And your human fears
     Of few tomorrows.

Your Majesty, although so stately,
With your path so strewn with flowers,
Praised with pomp and banner;
Kind and gentle manner,
     Mother of ours.

Your Majesty, for so many years
You've richly graced the royal scene
But under all the whirl,
We still discern the girl
     Of seventeen.

Hornby Island, 1995.08.18

Note: I sent the poem "Lovely, Lonely, Lady" to Her Majesty, Queen
Elizabeth The Queen Mother. The Lady-in-Waiting, Lady Margaret Colville,
wrote me a gracious letter of acknowledgement. It is not usual practice to
publish a personal letter of this kind, but the letter indicated that Queen
Elizabeth The Queen Mother was "touched" and expressed Her "sincere
thanks, together with warm appreciation".

Jane - at four

The Dancer

Dance - 'til your arms ache;
Dance - 'til all your muscles shake;
Dance - 'til sinews almost break;
        Dance!

Dance while the crowd hums;
Dance as the sweat runs;
Dance until the pain numbs;
        Dance!

Dance - though it gnarls your feet;
Dance - because the agony's sweet;
Dance - it makes your soul complete;
        Dance!

Dance by your mother's knee;
Dance when you're forty-three;
Dance, at last, in memory;
        Dance! Dance! Dance!

Hornby Island
1995.08.10

✳❤✳

Jack and Mollie Forster
Golden Wedding - 11 August 1995

This Plymouth lad and Bristol lass wed with eager passion
In the aftermath of war, with things still on the ration.
England, Scotland, Bishopbriggs, Weymouth, East Kilbride,
Were places that Jack lived and worked with Mollie by his side.
Inspections took him round the world
                  in cars and planes and ships;
Four kids they had in sixteen years -that's three extended trips!

In '62, Old Blighty's charms for Jack began to pall,
They gathered up their goods and chattels, sailed for Montreal.
Settled in Toronto, they couldn't ask for more,
'til Mollie gets the kids to watch - Jack's off to Labrador!

"Go west, young man!" the call soon came,
                  Vancouver beckons all;
Jack worked for Simons many years
                  while Richard still was small.
With them Jack sailed the seven seas
                  and braved the billows' foam
While Mollie held the fort they'd built
                  and raised the kids at home.

Another of Jack's many jobs was down in Argentina,
Where Mollie lived like Lady Muck -
                  my word, you should have seen her!
They'd go into a restaurant that finest steak dispenses,
The waiters gathered round like flies, for Jack was on expenses!

Jack's driving 's been a thrilling saga, Mollie will recall,
When he didn't drive her round the bend,
                  he drove her up the wall!
Jack's been in so many scrapes, the number staggers Mollie,
Some brought on by other folks,
                  but most through Jack's own folly.

One night to town they made their way
　　　　　　with George and Maureen Hood;
Jack argued with a driver and he landed on the hood!
The guy drove off with Jack still there,
　　　　　　spreadeagled on the bonnet,
At hectic speed till he fell off - his suit got dirt upon it!
Off Passage Island, lost his engine - on the rocks he blew;
Then home to Mollie dripping wet - and Maggie dripping too!
Mollie has our sympathy, for when she takes her ease,
In comes Jack with his face all black
　　　　　　and thick with engine grease!

Although Jack worked for Simons he
　　　　　　has also worked for Sandwell;
Some years before, he spilt much gore
　　　　　　when he cut off his hand well!
The doctors sewed it back at once, their efforts they'd redouble,
So Jack still uses both his hands to grab a hold of Trouble!

Though Jack has faults, he's thoughtful, kind,
　　　　　　and erudite as hell,
Strict with his kids, he's generous and treats his Mollie well.
Through eighteen thousand nights and days
　　　　　　they've lived and loved and fought.
How has their marriage lasted? Jack's been away a lot!
We all agree that 50 years is a long time looking back -
But it'd seem a darn sight longer if you'd had to live with Jack!

So raise your glasses, one and all, and give three hearty cheers
For Jack and Mollie Forster - married fifty years!

Hornby Island
1995.08.09

❄❤❄

The Little White Car That Cried

Once I had a little car, its paint was white as snow,
No matter where we ever went, the car was sure to go.
It was a Delta Eighty-eight, a handsome car and proud -
I would not have exchanged it
                              for a Rolls Royce Silver Cloud.
It wandered down the hill one day
                        without my wife and me;
The silly creature didn't stop until it struck a tree.
How this had happened, I'll relate - a sorry tale of woe
Of how our car had wandered where it wasn't meant to go.

One night, in bed, we heard a noise - it sounded like a car
Crunching on the gravel where the weeds and poppies are.
I rushed out to the car port and had a look around;
I ran to seek it down the drive but couldn't hear a sound.
We'd gone to bed and settled down, never heard a crash,
The little car had flown the coop
                        - what could I say but "Dash!".
At first I thought my little car was stolen by a thief,
Then saw its shadowed whiteness
                              where the car had come to grief.
What could we do but wring our hands
                        and then go back to bed,
Grieving for our little car - we feared that it was dead!

"Darkness, darkness, flee away!" - the night would never stop
- We'd call the car's insurers and we'd have to call a cop
And then a towtruck, harsh, uncaring, with its ropes of steel
- I could just imagine how our little car would feel!
Scraping, grinding, no one minding, but my wife and me,
Wrecking rhododendrons where the car had wrecked the tree.
Twinkle, twinkle, little car, all through the long, long night;
The cedar branches scraped its paint and gave it such a fright.
It lay there that eternal night, alone but for the deer
Who ate the rhododendrons - and their munching hurt its ear.

My car looked so dejected when they brought it up the slope,
But happy, yet, to see us both - it never quite lost hope.
It knew that it had run away and was itself to blame
And knew its Mum and Dad would surely use a nasty name.
But we were both too worried then
                to do much more than frown -
We'd feared we'd have to have the silly, little car put down.
We'd had it many years, you see, and loved it fond and true
And much preferred its glossy coat, white, not black and blue.
So now we have a little wedge, the car just loves it so -
It nestles fondly by the wheel and never lets it go.

One happy note, one person's pleased -
                its Mummy's special friend -
She treats her car so badly - it's all bashed from end to end.
Now, every time she hurts the car and it gets a little scrape
She says "I didn't wreck the thing and knock it out of shape"!
The moral of the story is, before to bed you take,
Make sure your little car's in "park"
                and you've applied the brake;
For if you don't, you'll rue its loss for many, many years
You'll lose insurance discounts and be red around the ears!

                    Hornby Island
                    1995.08.04

✳❤✳

Bob Woodley

Aesthetic, smiling, gentle man,
Loved and healed his fellow man;
Explosive laugh, expressive features,
Relished life and all its creatures.
Slender as his violin's bow
As nice a guy you'd ever know;
With such a bright blue eye.
   No chance to say goodbye.

Hornby Island
1995.07.30

I Love Thee, Life

I love thee, Life, and sip the cup
Of happiness that's offered up -
But, seeking fortune, fame, renown,
I haven't time to gulp it down.

Sister, brothers, friends and others,
Lovers past, and wife of mine,
A glass of port, a piece of cheese,
The pleasure sharing mellowed wine.

Even work at engineering -
All its challenge just adds spice,
Sunshine, woods, a sunny clearing,
Rain and snow and glittering ice.

That time is short should give us pause
And only flimsy curtains lie
Between us and the dragon's claws.
We may not know the "how" or "why"
But always have the time to die.

Hornby Island
1995.07.28

✳❤✳

Colin in Salamis, 1955

Cyprus

The leaves in the trees are waving a greeting
The scent on the breeze brings a memory, fleeting,
    Of a far-away island I knew
    A jewel in a setting of blue,
    Where melons and oranges grew.
Each stone held the spirit of ancients entreating
    The stranger to stop and recall
    The grandeur of palace and hall.

The pillars of Salamis, weathered and tumbled,
Stone blocks on the hillsides, all scattered and jumbled,
    Whisper from out of the mists
    "Though Nature herself still persists,
    However each princeling resists,
The swaggering trappings eventually crumbled."
    Leaving us here to enjoy
    Our instant of summer - and joy.

Hornby Island
1995.07.27

❤

Flirtation

The car was so crowded you sat on his knee
I sat in the seat just behind.
I don't recall where the party had been -
The thought's in the depths of my mind.

With your arm on his shoulder, you laughed in his ear;
I could sense how he warmed to your touch;
Sensual, provocative, gettable, near -
And I hated him ever so much.

I glimpsed your sweet breast in the vee of your dress
And felt his rapacious hot glance
And horror-struck watched him reach out for your breast -
Why not, when you gave him the chance?

I reached for your shoulders and begged you to cease,
Afraid where the petting might lead,
But from your reactions you'd do as you please
However I'd argue or plead.

I'd try one more time - just pretend not to care;
Said "Fuck it!" and then turned away.
You laughed, said "Yes please!" and then ruffled his hair.
"Oh Jane, Jane!" was all I could say.

I woke from the dream with my face wet with tears,
My heart simply pounding with hot, jealous fears.

Hornby Island
1995.07.10

England, This England

The Oxford dictionary states that "England"'s derivation
Is the French word "Angleterre"- not direct translation,
A corruption of the word by folk (perhaps of lower station?).

Let's now review some history and consider 5 AD:
Angles settled in the north,
 from Father Thames to River Forth
So this so-called translation could perhaps be a mutation
Of "Engla land" where the "Engla" part
 is the genitive form which has its start
In the nominative "Engli", changed from "Angle"
By Father Time - a positive tangle!

Instead of all this word pollution
I suggest a new solution:
We know that Angles cleared the woods
And in the fields then sowed their crops.
(Were they the ones that invented roods
 and drank the beer they made with hops?)
They, like many another nation,
Were sure to practise crop rotation
In which in every fallow year
A field becomes a meadow
(An awkward word, I fear,
For nothing rhymes, though meadow grass
Will surely fatten fallow deer).

Move on some years to 8 AD, then came the lusty Vikings
Who found the meadows there displayed
 were greatly to their likings.
They crushed resistance, liked the place
 and many settled down
And gave the language many a verb
 and many a simple noun.
And then they wrote to tell their friends
 of their former Viking band
To travel south and then turn right
 then straight to "Meadow Land".

Now we come to the vital part
- and this is a true translation,
For "eng" or "äng" means "meadow"
to the people of that nation.
They'd named the place in the same old way
they'd named so many before
Like Iceland, Greenland, Shetland, Vinland
- And I am sure there are several more.

So "England" just means "meadow land",
A simple derivation
Arising from the Angles through their love of cultivation
Then through the Vikings with their yen
for violent occupation.
The word would apply to all the land,
Not just the fields of the Angle,
But the meadows and marks and the fine shady parks
Where the Jute and the Saxon entangle.
Not "Angleterre" as Oxford says, which only goes to show
One can get too smart with the culture part
As wiser persons know.

Hornby Island
1995.07.01

Freedom of Speech

The Hornby Islander's freedom of speech
Is in danger, I declare.
I couldn't believe what I read last month -
I near fell off my chair!
The July First Edition
Borders on sedition,
Demands the next rendition
Of folks like me, who're fancy free
And write of the swallow, the flower and the bee,
Should confine our theme to the arty scene
Which caters in part to the cultured cream
Of Hornby's population!
This was not a sweet sensation!

❤

I suppose I could write of The Hall at night
With its crowds of folks sharing simple jokes
The massive stove's cast-iron yokes,
The mossy shakes and raisin cakes
Served with wine which the crowd partakes
Before each concert starts.
(This rhymes quite well in parts!)

But no - I refuse, and like others, I choose
To write each poem, till the cows come *hoem*
(To where?)
As I know I've always done
About any old subject under the sun.
So there!

Hornby Island
1995.07.01

Photo: Bob Cain

Hornby Island Community Hall

✳❤✳

The Ubiquitous Nose

Look around - they're all around -
Shapes and sizes all abound.
Colours, textures, straight or flexured,
Tiny, like a button,
Pink and shiny, purple, blue,
Aristocratic, like a shoe,
Or a piece of mutton!

Bulbous, pointed, aquiline,
Reddened with the sun,
Nostrils flaring, laughter sharing,
Twitching, full of fun.

Some are pierced, with rings and things,
Diamonds, pearls and rubies,
Hard to blow them, I would guess,
(This, the owners won't confess!)
Some, like sausage, some, like cukes
And some, like jubie-jubies.

Some are sniffed disdainfully
And tossed up in the air
Some are vented violently
And stuffed with nasal hair.

When you're small, they're ofttimes hurt
In rough and tumble games,
In the park or in the hall
And you bump them when you fall;
Red and bloody, often muddy,
And others call them names.

When you're bigger, they're more fun
And easier to tend,
They're lots of fun when snuggling
With a very special friend.

The basic concept's pretty sound -
Points downwards like a drain -
If it pointed upwards then
We'd drown out in the rain!

Hornby Island, 1995.06.24

A Chance To Dream

Sitting on a mower,
Round and round the field I go.
If it went any slower,
I would fall asleep, I know.

The motor's constant rumble
Filters through the plugs I wear.
Castles rise and crumble,
Edifices in the air.

There's a heady dreaming
Nurtured by the mower's sound.
Sunlight steady streaming
Warms my back each time around.

The engine's steady thrumming
Conjures up the songs I know -
Songs just made for humming,
Songs of love - and songs of woe.

Sitting here and brooding
On life's ephem'ral mystery -
Reality intruding -
Now it's done and time for tea!

Hornby Island
1995.05.02

Opinion

I'm an old insomniac,
I get my sleep in patches,
But not a sexual maniac,
Though I've torrid dreams in snatches.

Hornby Island
1995.05.01

❤

The Last Seduction

This movie, made by Astral Films,
 of USA, down south -
One message was - "Don't like your friends?" -
Just belt them in the mouth!

The major part, a woman, was horrid, simply evil,
Her heart was clearly poisoned
 by a large tobacco weevil.
She'd chain smoke, she'd manipulate,
She'd cheat and lie and kill,
She didn't trust a man who loved her -
Urged him on to kill
Her husband. He sold drugs, was violent,
 quite without remorse.
She eventually murdered him,
 when she was at her worst.

Dripping glamour, fancy clothes,
 cars and swigging scotch,
The best part of a man for her
 was the bit around his crotch.

The sex was ugly, violent, bleak,
 with not a taste of bliss,
All thrusting, shoving, nothing loving,
 every poisoned kiss.

Why teach our kids that evil triumphs,
 life's an empty shell
Of cheating, hating, fornicating,
 shooting, violence, hell?

I didn't have the guts to rise
 and walk out of the hall
And still don't know why a film like that
 was ever made at all.

Hornby Island
1995.04.29

✳❤✳

Night Travellers

When we kiss, the world stops turning
Stars and planets fade from view.
Lying, lovely, washed in moonlight,
My world contracts to only you.

Rounded breast and curving shoulder,
Sexy hip and lissom thigh,
In the shadow, hot lips parted,
Burning glance and sparkling eye.

The magic of the perfumed garden
Works its wonders in the dark,
Through the open window streaming,
Urging lovers to embark
On that familiar wanton journey,
Ripples spreading on a pond,
Feelings bursting ever outward,
Through the stargate and beyond.

Hornby Island
1995.04.29

✳❤✳

The Dandelion King

In caverns measureless to man,
Where Alph the sacred river runs,
There rules a mighty personage
That all of us should fear.
He sits upon a golden throne
And, in his hand, not skin, nor bone,
He wields a multi-prongèd spear.

He rages as we mow the grass
And sees his scattered minions fall.
He sends them reinforcements
Who stand there, proud and tall,
Waving to their fallen comrades,
Changed to fairy down,
Swept upon the winds of spring
And settling on the garden
In a frothy, snowy pall.

He jabs his spear like lightning bolts
The multi-tips all flashing,
Challenging us earthly dolts
Who garden here, above.
Each stab exhorts another legion
To invade another region
That we thought was safe from harm.
Field and meadow, shaded woodland,
Gardens, all are conquered by
His all-embracing arm.

To our alarm, there comes a time
With every single dandelion,
There comes a golden buttercup!
Why bother then to cut them down
Or even dig them up.
Walt disnae!

Hornby Island
1995.04.29

❋♥❋

Tourists in a Dream

The castle walls were creamy in the sunshine,
The grass beside the keep was brightly green,
As Mum and I walked, laughing,
        through the courtyards
Of a castle that the world has never seen.

I looked around for treasure on the walls there;
Sought silver goblets in the vaults below;
Found battered bucklers and a trusty broadsword
And a lady's ring, perhaps from long ago.

The waking brought nostalgia flooding over,
The morning gloaming's silence was complete,
As I recalled the wonder of that visit
To that castle and my mother's joyful feet.

Hornby Island
1995.04.23

✼❤✼

Fantasies

Life is simple, undramatic,
 a cheerful loving round,
Eating, walking, loving, talking,
 pleasantries abound.
I work a bit, and fetch the mail,
 do a little chore,
Walk the beach, and hear the seagulls,
 watch the eagles soar.

Out of the blue,
 I hear your voice and sunny laughter,
Feel your loving hand, here,
 warmly nestled into mine.
One of the questions
 that will torture me hereafter -
Are your honeyed kisses
 still as warm and sweet as wine?

These fantasies, these images,
 come with sudden poignancy,
Memories of a younger age,
 a loving girl and boy.
Regretfully, I shut them out,
 them I can't permit,
An eighteen-year relationship
 to wantonly destroy.

Hornby Island
1995.04.22

＊♥＊

Dawn - 9 April 1995

From a lonely hotel room in Derby,
I beheld a fox,
Not thirty feet from my window,
Prowl a winding grassy path,
Saw a sunburst of shimmering daffodils
Detected the doves' gentle loving call.

Then, near Cloudwood Close,
As the sun came up,
Wan in the morning mist,
I heard a blackbird's golden song of Joy.

Derby
1995.04.09

✳❤✳

Regret

It's thirty years since last we met,
Since last I called you, Vera, "Pet",
So warm in memory - and yet
So very long ago.
It seems I'll never quite forget,
And wanted you to know.

You may have never thought of me,
But I have thought, my dear, of thee,
In sudden haunting memory,
A glimpse from time to time,
Of things that could not ever be
Just simply yours and mine.

I rang - the years just slipped away -
I heard your laugh, so light and gay,
I saw the sweet expressions play
Across your gentle face.
Sun dappled woods, the scent of May,
Another time and place.

I fantasized - a way of mine -
Of things we'd do, your eyes would shine.
I never dreamed that you'd decline,
That Life could be so cruel.
Instead of being your Valentine
I'm just your April Fool!

I hope by now you will have seen
I never meant to be so mean,
Let me explain each tangled skein
And not repent it -
The lovers that we could have been,
Had Fate but meant it.

Berlin, West Germany
1995.04.07

❤

Eastern Turbot Crisis? Western Herring Tragedy!

The turbot crisis makes me sick -
Pardon me for swearing -
Canadians speak with forkèd tongue -
Save the turbot - bugger the herring!

The Lambert Channel teemed with life -
The gulls were massed along the shore
Raucous, feisty, full of strife,
Participants in Spring's encore!
Stellar sea lions, harbour seals,
Plunged and rolled and dived around;
For weeks we'd heard them call with joy -
The nights were vibrant with their sound.
Eagles hovered, buzzards soared
In lazy circles slowly there,
Looking for the milky patterned
Water where the herring were.

Suddenly -
The fishboat engines grind and thunder,
Loaded down with silver plunder,
Roe - destined mostly for Japan,
To feed the face of greedy Man.

One week later, nothing stirs,
Most gulls have gone, the sealions fled,
Leaving us to ask the question -
Do the herring mourn their dead?

Murdered millions with no appeal -
And, on the beach, a headless seal.

Hornby Island
1995.03.23

Note: The seal was actually a sea lion, probably weighing about three
hundred pounds; the head had been cut off cleanly and there were no
other injuries on the body.

✳❤✳

Two's Company

Oh, I love to hear you snore
And rattle the hinges on the door!
Think how lonely it would be
With no one there to snore but me!

Hornby Island
1995.03.10

Close Encounter

Wakening,
Listening,
Starlight glistening.
Lying dreaming,
Moonlight streaming.

Silent and warm,
My love sleeps?
Her hand meets mine,
My heart leaps.

Hornby Island
1995.03.10

✳❤✳

Douglas Muir

Douglas trips the light fantastic,
       quite fantastic, slim and neat;
Even when there is no music,
       he can't still his twinkling feet!

Polished, in his kilted splendour,
       he's the one to beat the band,
Now he's seventy, one year closer
       to that distant Promised Land
Of non-stop Scottish Country Dancing,
       music sweet as Orpheus made,
Where he'll dance on floors of gold
       and angels serve up lemonade!.

                Hornby Island
                1995.03.06

Photo: Bob Cain

Hornby Island Snow

The snow that came in early March,
down from the Island hills
Covered all the crocuses
and bent the nodding daffodils.

The beauty of the flowering plum,
proud in its springtime spree,
By sparkling snow on shrub and tree,
was matched in all its tracery.

The robins forage in the leaves,
crackling and free from snow
Under branches trimmed with white,
where April lilies slowly grow.

The bees are banished to their beds,
snug in their snow-decked hives,
While we wait, eternally,
until our second spring arrives.

Hornby Island
1995.03.05

✳❤✳

No Wonder!

Six billion bits of information
Locked up in that complex strand
    Of DNA.
One six-billionth - no sensation -
On Tribune Bay, one grain of sand -
    A part to play!

But one-six-billionth is no trifle -
Means you're ugly - or an eyeful -
    Or straight or gay!

No wonder we're so very different
Don't always see just eye to eye,
    Surprise, surprise!

One little bit makes crows-feet crinkle,
One creates delicious wanting,
    Or loving cries.
That subtle smile, that hateful wrinkle,
And that shade of green, enchanting,
    In your lovely eyes.

               Hornby Island
               1995.03.04

✳❤✳

Death Sits on Mummy's Lap

The other day a little car was headed for the ferry,
Mum and Dad all belted up -
      but Baby, where was she?
They're off to spend a day in town
      to make a little merry!
Sitting perched on Mummy's lap
      for all the world to see
Their child was sat all happily
      on Mummy's loving knee,
"Protected" by her tender arms
      and smiled contentedly.

Now, Death just loves the loaded dice.
Death prepares that patch of ice.
Death loves that child on Mummy's knee -
He loves a funeral, you see.

A little skid, Dad can't control,
A yawning ditch, a Hydro pole,
A horrid fishtail - sickening glide -
A child that weighs two hundred pounds,
A cannonball that's fired inside
      That happy little car.

I hope they made it safely home -
I hope they read this little poem.
I hope next time that child will sit,
Buckled up, not free to roam,
In spite of every shrill protest
- Then Death will shoot his dice alone.

                Hornby Island
                1995.03.03

❤

The Last Straw?

The sky was red that morning -
　　it should have been a warning!
Birthday - fifty-nine today - took a trip to Courtenay -
Caught the early ferry. Just to buy some sherry?
No - gin and brandy, rum and scotch,
　　to celebrate that extra notch
(The scotch was not for me!)

Driver's licence to renew, picture out of focus too -
Maybe just my eyes. Wind is on the rise;
Raining now and sky as black as hell -
　　Oh well - have a nasty hunch
　　that we'd better hasten lunch -
The ferry may be cancelled - who can tell?

So - swig our wine and gulp our lunch
　　and then we rush around!
Went to buy a piece of china for a former flame -
"Sorry, sir - it's out of stock." said the counter dame.

Rain like bullets, colder too, maybe snowing soon,
Visions of the ferry sinking, battered by typhoon!
Pharmasave to buy some cards, hastily we park,
Raincoat's getting sodden and the sky is really dark!

Made it to the ferry - four o'clock, by just a minute,
Got my glasses' case, but there ain't no glasses in it!
　　Bugger - hot around the collar -
　　there goes another hard-earned dollar!

We don't get on the ferry - two other cars and us -
We watch the kids all rushing on,
　　from that yellow bus!
Another hour to wait. Tough!
How's the crossing? Rough!

Felt rather glum.
But - worse to come!
One more tragedy in store,
- did I deserve all this - and more?
In the mirror that night - just glittering there -
In my left eyebrow, a shining white hair!

Happy Birthday to You!

Hornby Island
1995.02.25

Reflections on a New Tombstone

My father died at sixty-three, my Uncle Jack at 58 -
Now I'm fifty-nine myself - it's young
    to knock at the Pearly Gate!

"Hey Jimmy - " says Death, "come along wi' me!
Ye've nae time fer yer cup o' tea -
therr's a wan wey trip aheed!"
(You'll note that rhymes with "deid".)

Bargain a bit - "Hey Death - wait up -
give me a minute to savour the cup -
sit down - have a rest - don't work so hard!
Just give me the time to tidy the yard,
clear the blackberry patch, fix that faulty latch -
just a few more days at home -
write that last great epic poem!"

Does he hear you? No. When he comes - you go!
Mops you up like ink with a blotter -
Then you're off on that trip with a stiff upper lip
And leave a few scribbled notes in your jotter!
Some mould'ring reports, a patent or two -
Worth about as much as the smoke inside the flue -
Some paintings - there's one of my wife
one summer on Hornby - some poems, some songs
- Is this all I did with my life?

I've looked at the sunsets, and gazed at the stars
Seen Jupiter's moons, identified Mars,
Thrown stones in the ocean, strolled on the shore,
Passed my genes to my kids -
      is there really much more
I should want - to recall?

There's regret that I didn't do more.

Danced till my feet fell off, Saturday night,
The Majestic, The Highlanders, The Plaza's delight,
      My badminton frenzy lasted some years
Until my heart's fluttering gave me a fright!
So many books to read, so many songs to sing,
Girls that I've loved in the winter and spring -
Hand-in-hand by the river, arm-in-arm on the shore,
A hug on a hillside, a kiss at the door -
      Fond memories, all.

          Hornby Island
          1995.02.02

❋♥❋

The Voyageurs

Who knows what casual Fate may bring
This fragile globe on which we sing
Our plaintive little song?
It only takes a climate change
Too great for life to rearrange
Its ways, to come along!

It may be that we'll detect
A world so large we can't deflect
It from our rendezvous.
And then, our sun will surely grow
Its fiery disk will overthrow
Our earth of emerald hue!

Some great volcano's sudden gout
Of dust and smoke can snuff us out
Like candles in the breeze!
Our future lies across the gulf
Of stars that guided Leif and Ulf
Across the trackless seas.

Our seed will fly in silver craft
Down every starry way,
Long after our last laugh is laughed
And Earth is molten clay.
I see the minarets and towers
Of wondrous worlds remote from ours
Where our descendants play.

Hornby Island
1995.01.11

❤

Magical Moment

What a lovely show! The sky was all a-glow,
The sun was going down and it wanted us to know
That it wasn't finished yet.

We were swimming there;
there were diamonds in your hair -
Droplets all a-glitter from the sun-god's golden flare
Where the sun and skyline met.

The sea was summer soft and smooth,
and cradled me and you,
Cool upon our skin.
The trees, so far a-loft, were still,
bright green against the blue.
Remote, the ferry din.

And then -
that magic moment when the sun dips down -
A golden-outlined cloud where the sun had been -
A moment when I held you close, still lissom, brown -
As lovely as the sunset we had seen.

Hornby Island
1994.08.16

❤

Brief Encounter in a Perseid Meteor Shower

A satellite was cruising,
        musing he was rivalling the stars.
Just a garbage can with wings,
        and other shiny things,
His reflection was like Jupiter or Mars.

There came a shooting star, wand'ring from afar,
Like a comet trailing fire in every feature.
When he met the satellite in the breathless starry night,
What could he say, but - "Well - I'm pleased to meteor!"

The satellite couldn't speak - because he'd sprung a leak.
        In addition, he received a dreadful fright.
As he rocketed away, he heard the meteor say
    In a tinkly rhyme - "Goodnight, sweet satellite!"

        Far above the Lambert Channel,
            he stuffed a piece of flannel
        In the hole the star had made,
            though this wasn't in the manual
And made a swift repair in the accidental tear -
But he felt a little silly with the flannel hanging there.

There's a message here for us as we wander in the dust
        And gaze up to the cosmos with its dangers -
All that glitters is not gold in the heavens' starry fold
- And listen to your Mum - don't speak to strangers!

                    Hornby Island
                    1994.08.15

✳❤✳

To Ted Walker - On His Eightieth Birthday

For someone as youthful as I,
It's hard to imagine why
There should be so much fuss
Over one so much older than us?

Your lim'ricks, we love 'em - keep churning them out!
Your cartoons are fantastic - whate'er they're about!
Your project to publish those pics of New York
Is as thrilling as greeting a child-laden stork!

So - knowing you - the reason's quite clear!
Here's to another exciting year!

Hornby Island
1994.07.02

Islands in the Sun

If every man is an island,
The one I'd like to be
Would have to be Hornby Island
Where the air is fresh and free.

Then you'd be Denman Island -
By my side you'd make me thrill,
And when comes the time that the seas dry up
Then we'd be closer still.

Hornby Island
1994.06.22

Sweet Wild Rose

Traveller, with your blinkered eye
And dusty, worldly shoe,
I see you as you hurry by
And wonder what you do.

Your days are filled with empty toil,
Your nights - too tired to woo -
You steam along at rolling boil
But Life holds more for you,
You fool - consider this today -
You never have the time to play;
November quickly follows May.

Sweet rose, I glimpse you, barely hear your tiny song.
Things superficial tug us, inexorably along.
And perhaps I'm just afraid to linger here at all
To see the crocus wither, and your petals as they fall.

Hornby Island
1994.06.09

Health Hint

Though people thay that grapefruit pith
Is found to be of uthe
In fighting your cholethterol -
I think they mean the juthe!

Hornby Island
1994.04.21

✳❤✳

Happy Birthday To You!

"Forty, Forty, Forty, Forty" rings the knell of Doom!
It'll do the same at fifty
with a more resounding "Boom"
And then the same at seventy - and eighty, too, I fears
- But I'm damned if I will listen
and I'll plug up both my ears!

Now that sixty's coming round
it brings a new perspective -
My body's quietly going to seed - it's partially defective.
I now wear specs - I've other aches
I never used to know -
I've now got "trigger finger" - next comes "trigger toe"?
"Trigger cock" would be more fun
But that's not meant to be!
I've got a minor tremor in my eyeball and my knee.
But I, still, defiantly,
await that trumpet sound -
By the time that seventy comes along
I may be underground!
So, cheer up, Mac, and cut the corn,
and steal a rose or two
Before The Reaper comes along
and rudely pinches you!

> West Vancouver
> 1975.08.26
> and
> Hornby Island
> 1994.04.21

❉❤❉

The Piano

My former music teacher would surely have flipped
Had she seen "The Piano" we saw -
The fine Scottish accents would give her a lift
And for sure now, the music was braw!

That New Zealand beach with its wild boiling surf
Was dramatic as any she'd see,
While the settlers plod on, indomitably,
With the mud splashing over their knee.

But the bit where the Maori stood naked and tall
And the maiden slipped out of her dress
Would have brought out a blush
                 on her parchment-like cheek
And quickened her breathing, I guess!

She'd have rushed to her piano and taken a key
And sent it off straight to a friend,
Determined to savour the sins of the flesh
Before her life came to an end.

Then he'd scurry round, and with her "A chord",
Would wrestle her down to the floor.
She'd emulate all of the things that she'd seen
And urgently beg him for more!

So - all you old fellows that once laughed at me
As I sped to my sweet music lesson -
You'll envy the things that we did in that room
- Or maybe we didn't! Keep guessin'!

I've now got a piano that's harder to play
For a perfectly obvious reason -
I've sent half the keys to the girls of my choice
With the onset of each silly season!

                       Hornby Island
                       1994.04.21

♥

Bob Tipping

With his broad sleepy grin and the shrewdest of eyes
- he could move very quickly in spite of his size -
He liked to play tennis, he loved to drink wine,
But hockey was always his Cloud Number Nine.
He could argue and bargue, was always polite,
When he gave his opinion - 'twas probably right!
He would listen and ponder and just seem to dose,
Then give you the answer in erudite prose.

He'd sit in his chair, with an indolent air
- King Heron Rocks! It's true!
One New year's night - they were all quite tight -
He was King of Hornby too!

Bob was a truly gentle giant in every kind of way
And he played the Game of Life that only the fairest play.
I'll mourn Old Tip when his face pops up,
Out of the cloudless blue,
But, Pat, and Matt, and Julie - I really cry for you.

Hornby Island
1994.04.20

❋❤❋

Photo: Bob Cain

Heron Rocks, Hornby Island

❤

Pleasures of the Flesh?

Need to pee a bit more often,
Want to screw a little less,
Looms the outline of the coffin,
Abbreviated happiness!

Life comes sharply into focus,
All the trivia fall away,
Just when I had come to think that
Happiness was here to stay!

Fateful lump upon my prostate,
From the shadows of my mind?
Maybe just a slight infection?
Pray that Fortune is so kind!

Eyesight, hearing, slowly failing,
Pleasures of the flesh curtailing.

Hornby Island
1994.04.04

❋❤❋

Crisis - Solution

I'm down on the beach for a walk with the dog,
The wife turns to speak and she slips on a log.
She turns and she twists and she lies, oh, so still -
     Uh-oh - what do I do?

I'm out in the kitchen preparing a meal
The children are quiet, then one gives a squeal.
I run through to see - blood - all over the floor -
     Uh-oh - what do I do?

We're going to the school and the kids start to race;
One child collapses, turns blue in the face;
I can't feel her pulse and don't feel her breathe -
     Uh-oh - what do I do?

In these situations the victim is *dead*
In three or four minutes is what the man said.
Your action is vital, you cannot just say
     "Uh-oh - what do I do?"

If *you* think you're helpless and quite at a loss,
Then *you* need a course from the famous Red Cross.
It just takes a couple of hours of your time -
     Then you'll know what to do.

Hornby Island
1994.02.15

✽❤✽

Breath-taking

Did *you* see the moon last morning,
The sky in the west adorning,
Enhancing the blue of the dawning clear,
Which came with the first sharp frost of the year?

The hills, bright green, with their tops of snow,
Pure and white, with a dazzling glow -
But the Lambert Channel, most striking of all,
Was calm and smooth as the floor of a hall
In Heaven - a surface of silvery light,
Not from the moon, but the sky so bright -
And there from the moon on the crest of the hill,
Balancing, ancient, timeless and still,
The same today as in days of old,
Came a broad bright path of burnished gold.

Hornby Island
1994.01.28

Sandy Thompson

We knew you a moment, Blithe Sandy -
So cheery, so witty, and bright -
But just for a brief shining instant,
Then you passed - like a ship in the night.

Hornby Island
1994.01.28

✳❤✳

The Proverbial Philanderer Comes Home

"Fools rush in
where guardian angels always fear to tread"
Was one of many homilies that kept me out of bed.
I always was the kind of guy
who looked before he leapt,
Which limited the kind of girls
with whom I'd gladly slept!

Take simple curiosity - we all are prone to that -
It made the chicken cross the road -
it also killed the cat.
The grass may well seem greener
on the fence's other side,
But the bird in the hand may compensate
for someone else's bride.

Although we know that half a loaf
will oftentimes suffice,
Though, once the loaf is started -
would one really miss a slice?
A miss is said to be as good as any travelled mile,
But isn't half as tempting as a mistress with a smile!

All that glitters is not gold - it may be simply frost -
But it doesn't pay to hesitate, for he who does is lost.
A pair of lacy panties lends enchantment to the view
To a rolling stone who gathers moss
quite happily with you!

Hornby Island
1993.12.25

❋❤❋

Moving Again

Moving again, lots of fun,
stress to beat the band!
Experience tells you - No.1 -
got to get it planned.

Fixing the date - not too tough -
check with all the boys.
Booking the truck, easy enough -
room for all our toys?

Boxes to get, that's a chore -
they take up so much space.
China in piles, books on the floor,
Everything out of place.

Gardening stuff, all our books,
What are we trying to prove?
Must be mad - couple of kooks -
Maybe we shouldn't move!

Banish the thought, press right on -
pretend we're having fun!
Comes the day - pantechnicon -
Moving at a run!

Always it rains - ceaselesslee
miles from the door to the van!
Sandwich now, cups of tea -
Grab them while you can!

Loading all done - last look round
Whisk here and there with a broom.
Nostalgia reigns - an echoing sound
In every empty room.

Trucking along, up there, sat,
Trundling along the road.
What can go wrong? Maybe a flat?
Maybe a shifting load?

✳❤✳

Time to unload, full speed ahead,
The move's about complete.
Plate of soup, lovely bread,
's great to have a seat.

Back to the truck - feel just great -
We made short work of that!
Suddenly stop - pause at the gate -
Damn it all - where's the cat?

West Vancouver
1993.07.24

The Singing Sails

A beautiful line that I wish were mine
Was one that my Gran used to sing
Of a prince on the run in a bonny wee boat
That sped like a bird on the wing.

The sea rushes past, the wind sings in the mast
And coolly caresses my cheek
We rush down the slope of a watery hill
Then soar from the trough to the peak.

With the sun in the sky and the sea swirling by,
Foaming - right up to the rail,
With the deck heeling hard,
            there's a lump in my throat
As the wind sculpts the sweep of the sail.

Speed bonny boat like a bird on the wing
In that beautiful song that my Gran used to sing.

West Vancouver
1993.07.16

✳♥✳

Hard Rock Video

Ugly faces and squalid places,
Rampant sex and drugs and smoking,
Shifting scenes of sick shebeens -
It's hardly thought-provoking.

Screaming heads and mouths and faces,
Straining jeans and horrid creatures
Lacking all the social graces,
Coarseness in their loathsome features.

Phallic fiddles and grinding guitars,
Changing, dazzling, whining, frazzling,
Trashy trucks and macho cars,
Fans call these sub-humans, stars!
                    Yuck!

                    West Vancouver
                    1993.06.27

The Construction Worker's Lament

I walked past a hole, the other fine day,
Half a block long and as much the other way.
Ten metres deep (that's thirty-five feet!),
At the corner of Howe and Davie Street.

I looked in the pit and I saw then,
A bunch of wee fore-shortened men
Swirling now and then, like a bunch of crazy hens
In a concrete pit, like a black bear den,
   In a zoo, boo-hoo!

They were all down there, working merrily away,
Not for a buck - a two-hundred-dollar day!
Comes twelve noon and they all tools down
  And lunch at the best re-bar in town!
If it rains hard now, will those guys all drown?

Don't be so daft - they'll just get damp
And scurry up and hurry up that long steep ramp -
Or shin on up the wiring to that great big lamp.

I regret, I digress - gotta move right on
Like the work in this huge construction zone.
If you must have a fag, there's a quiet Big John.

There's a slim tall crane that sways around a lot
When the sun beats down then the cab gets hot.
It can get quite cold as it swings in the breeze -
Not too good for your wobbly (knobbly?) knees.
A walk on the jib makes your toenails curl
To cling to the jib - hope they won't uncurl!
To work up there is a thrill to some
With a view of the crew and to Kingdom Come
- If you fall - boo-hoo!

Don't think of that - or the big fat "splat" -
You in wet cement in your new hard hat!

A few more weeks and the hole's all gone.
The block takes shape, the job rolls on.
Windows come - and windows go -
There's always a not-too-careful Joe!

On goes the roof and the kitchens all arrive -
You can see this is nobody's squalid little dive.
All rich stuff, worth a nickel or two -
Not for the likes of poor old you!
It's all quite sad, now my tale is told -
You can't buy a flat 'cos they've all been sold!

West Vancouver
1993.06.22

Puget Sound Mood Shift

When I feel blue 'cos I can't see you
'Cos you've got a thousand things to do,
Then I take my lute or my old brass flute
And then play a mournful root-toot-toot
Of Puget Sound - Puget Sound.

It ain't so hot, but it's all I've got,
Just a catchy tune 'neath a lonely moon.
Starts deep and cool like a rainbow pool
With a trout deep down, like a distant jewel
In Puget Sound - Puget Sound.

Now it's more upbeat and I tap both feet
And I think of you and you look so sweet
In a summer dress, with your hair in a mess
And that pulse in your throat when we're out on a boat
On Puget Sound - Puget Sound!

The tune flies along and my fingers play a song -
I've flung away my shoes
and I've sung away my blues.
A million swallows in the air,
streaming ribbons in her hair -
Now my memory has caught her -
sunlight dancing on the water
Of Puget Sound - Puget Sound!

West Vancouver
1993.06.21

❊❤❊

Unbalanced?

If you've seen me lately
and I seem a little queer,
It's 'cause I'm having trouble
with my little inner ear.

Endolymphatic hydrops
deals with water in a tube;
The tube affects your balance
and you wobble like a boob!

It makes me downright queasy
when I turn my head around -
I'm down upon my hands and knees -
just inches from the ground!

The doctor gave me pinkish pills -
you'll not believe this true -
The side effects are dizziness
and nasty nausea too!

I wish they'd find the cure because
I don't like feeling sick -
especially since the thing affects
the workings of my - stomach!

West Vancouver
1993.04.25

❤

The Passing of Eva Lyons

The sun's dull ember barely brightens
The clouds that cloak the distant hills.
Here, on the shore, each heartstring tightens,
Each mind, the thought of Eva fills.

The dinghy lies upon the water,
Perhaps a hundred feet from shore.
A minute's quiet, her ashes scatter,
"Lord, give her peace", our hearts implore.

It seems to all that Time just froze
And no one stirred upon the strand.
The spell then broke, a blood-red rose
Was cast - a gift from every hand.

Then someone said, with rueful grin,
With luck, in Heaven, they'll serve her gin.

West Vancouver
1993.03.13

Ode To Crocuses

Your name's a shame, sweet little flowers
That decorate the springtime sod
With yellow, purple, snowy showers.
The man that named you was a clod!

A consolation it must be
To you on whom my ode now focuses,
And sweet revenge to know that he
Is surely pushing up the crocuses!

> West Vancouver
> 1993.02.15

❤ *My Valentine Love* ❤

How can I gauge my love for you?
Words can't describe its pleasures;
Language needs words all fresh and new.
Kings cannot count its treasures.

Out beyond boundless space and time
Galaxies swirl and cluster.
They've never seen such a love, sublime,
In the years that their aeons muster.

After the melted rocks have cooled,
Scorched by the suns above you,
So long will last my love, bejewell'd,
My Valentine, I love you.

> West Vancouver
> 1993.02.14

✳❤✳

Around A Haggis

Ballet dancin', prancin' Jane
Dresses sharply, never plain;
Loves her man and ony wean
      That's big or sma'
But fash her not - le'e well alane
      For then she'll claw!

Smokin', sparklin', Geordie Hood,
Was ne'er amang the unco' guid -
He loves a lass, he loves his food.
      Scotch helps him sing.
He puts abin' his boiler brood
      His gouffin' swing!

She's young inside, no' auld, Auld Mary
She dances light as ony fairy
Sings true and clear as yon canary,
      O' maids in garrets.
She likes her dram and wee bit sherry -
      And also, clarets.

Jackie's bright and Jackie's sprightly
And he'll fight or screw thrice nightly
Loves his boat, wave-dancing brightly.
      Betimes he'll moan.
Full gen'rous, but, when close, tread lightly -
      He's mishap-prone.

Fae darkest Glesca Maureen hails,
Her sparklin' e'e the sunshine pales
When George goes gowffin', then she rails
      - at least, she would,
But now, she to the dancin' sails
      - it does her guid.

Plump and comfortable Mollie
Wi' wit and tongue as sharp as holly
Wi' Scottish dancin' cronies jolly
      Gi'es Jack the slip.
Let him commit another folly -
      Gi'es Jack her lip!

✻❤✻

Bald, quick of wit and elbow too,
He disna' mean nae hurt to you.
Precise in grammar - mak's ye gru.
    And loves the lasses.
Ye'll hear Col'n sing and whistle too
    Whene'er he passes.

The haggis came, the haggis went,
Wi' drink enough to drown a saint
Companions a', we'd one complaint
    - That Time goes on.
A few more years we're a' hell-bent -
    Or spirits, Mon!   Guid health!

        West Vancouver
        1993.01.24

*To Some Folk Who Should Have Been
Around A Haggis - But Caught The 'Flu*

I had writ' a rhyme for you
Tae read ayont the haggis stew
That Jane had made wi' veggies too
    Tae mak' ye groan.
Too bad ye went and caught the 'flu!
    So get well soon!

When Nickie's down, the world looks black,
He looks for Doomsday's final crack.
The big day in the almanac
    - Friday thirteen!
But cannie, couthie, kind wee mac;
    Eyes - hazel-green.

Anither Glesca Maureen sate
In auld Bearsden in worldly state
She didnae want tae emigrate.
    Vancouver? Nay!
Now she thanks her kindly fate
    And thinks she'll stay.

＊❤＊

Such rhymes are meant tae read when fu'
O' food an' drink an' haggis too.
Ye canna tak' offence when you
    Are feelin' swell.
I hope they're just as funny noo
    That ye're no' well!

The words come rollin' down the glen -
It only happens now and then,
But when it does, I tell ye, then
    I have tae write them!
The sword is weaker than the pen -
    Ye canna fight them!

West Vancouver
1993.01.24

Crows In A Storm

The snow was driving from the east,
'Twas blowing half a gale at least.
I sat and watched the other day -
Some crows had found a place to play.

The wind would strike the building face
And, driving upward, swiftly race
In powerful gusts up to the sky.
The crows would come and bravely fly
    Into the upward blast.
They'd scatter, swoop and flutter up.
The air was full - they clutter'd up
    The sky as time went past.

So now I feel that I can say
I've seen some dinosaurs at play!

West Vancouver
1993.01.24

❤

Geological Time Scale Mnemonic
Cenozoic, Mesozoic, Palaeozoic, etc.)

Eras first, then the periods:
        Can Man, Perpetually Pro-creating,
        Quell The Consumers' Joyful Tide,
        Perhaps Preventing Mass-destruction,
        Dreadful, Selfish, Owners Chide?

Then the epochs of the Cenozoic era:
        Recycling Playthings Plainly Massages
        Our Evolving Pride!

                West Vancouver
                1992.11.19

Location, Location, Location - 1808 Duchess Avenue

    Sold up on 11th Street - we could have run
    To leisure on Hornby and sunshiny fun.
    House prices kept falling - a spiralling twist.
    The prospect of profit was hard to resist.

    A shabby old house, a scabby old house,
    With cracks in the ceilings and traces of mouse!
    But above everything, what a location!
    (It gave me a positive profit sensation!)

    Two blocks from Safeway, and buses in reach,
    Across from the Legion and near to the beach.
    If we have a heart attack down by the foam,
    It's handy for Hollyburn Funeral Home.

    If your Tontine fun'ral is held before ours,
    We'll get you a discount at West Vancou' Flowers!

                West Vancouver
                1991.02.02

✳❤✳

September Song in Kilmartin, Argyll

Every hour, on the hour,
Just like clockwork, it would seem
Comes a real' torrential shower,
Filling every ditch and stream.

In between, the light is lovely;
The views are gorgeous every day,
But, with this rainfall, it's surprising
The standing stones aren't washed away!

Hurricane Gustav was then the excuse
For the heavens to open and rain like the deuce!
The sun was a mem'ry, the rain battered down
And leaves blew off wildly, like ripe thistledown.

The lesson we learned when we come back next year,
Is to pack rubber boots and our wet weather gear!

Kilmartin
1990.09.12

✻❤✻

Happy Days - Jim Porter's Retirement

Ev'n if it's raining, it's sure to be fine!
I'm taking retirement - it's holiday time!

On dark winter mornings, I'll turn over and snooze.
For cheap entertainment I'll make my own booze!

A day at the races is well within reach;
Or maybe I'll just spend a day at the beach.

I'll maybe go gliding and soar with the gulls;
I'll maybe go riding and chase all the girls!

There's always tomorrow for cutting the grass;
When I'm in retirement I'll sit on my - seat in the sun!

Ev'n if it's raining, it's sure to be fine!
I'm taking retirement - it's holiday time!

West Vancouver
1990.06

Homily

Not to waste paper's a sensible caper!
Go and do likewise and you can economize!

West Vancouver
1990.01

✳❤✳

Colin, Rhyming-on-the-drunken-spot

I have to apologise
For not having a rhyme;
Just to soliloquise,
I've not had the time.

It seems that the Tontine
Is rolling along;
Our members are healthy,
Hearty and strong.

How can I tell you
That I'm feeling blue?
We're all so damned healthy -
Too good to be true!

Wine, women and song
Will finish us off -
Or - for those of us smokers -
That insidious cough!

Vancouver 1990.03.03

Student Blues
(From "Vancouver Playground", a musical I was working on)

I can make a cup of coffee last all night.
Sitting, chatting with my friends I feel just right.
It isn't that I'm miserly or simply tight -
It's just that I've got no money!

Chorus: Student blues, student blues!
You wouldn't want to travel in my old worn shoes!
Student moans, student groans -
But most of them are rectified by student loans!
Deep in debt? Not just yet!
I hope the price of coffee stays the same!

I like this place because I get to sit and blab
And also 'cause there's never an outrageous tab.
The risk is I accumulate a lot of flab
From eating shortcake with honey!

I like to see the pictures here upon the walls;
Rather more exciting than ancestral halls.
It's always very diff'rent and it never palls
 And some of it is downright funny!

The waitresses have always got a pleasant smile,
Even when you sit here for a long, long, while,
The kind of girls you'd spot from nearly half a mile -
 And I know they're not after my money!

Vancouver
1988.07.03

The Conspirators' Polka
(From "Vancouver Playground")

(Burn the Town and Blow the Bridge!)

All the sparks whirl from the fire
With a lovely crackling sound
And we'll watch the flames go higher
As the city burns to the ground.
And when the smoke clears in the morning
From the glowing piles of ash,
Then we won't be wearing mourning
'Cause we're gonna make piles of cash!

Chorus:

We hope you'll all excuse our tizziness,
But we're going to make lots of dough,
And the ways we boost our business
Nobody will ever know!

There will be a great explosion
And the bridge will come tumbling down
And some bits will fall in the ocean
And some pieces fall in the town.
When the girders all have landed,
We'll take the champagne from the fridge,
For it won't be for long we're stranded,
We'll get a super new six-lane bridge!

We've got a large and fast old Chevy
To ensure that we can speed away
So that we can all catch the ferry
In the harbour at Horseshoe Bay.
We've explosives by the casefull
We've got detonators too;
The bang will be quite disgraceful
And they'll hear it in Timbuktu!

Yes, there's been a miscalculation
And we're all going to go to jail
But we're glowing with anticipation
'Cause we're bound to get out on bail!
Then we'll blow a few more bridges
And we'll burn down another town
- It's harder than catching midges
To keep a really good baddy down!

Hornby Island
1988.07.28

Come and Dance with Me
(From "Vancouver Playground")

Chorus:
I love to dance, you see,
Because my heart is free;
So why don't you come along and dance with me.
If you'd dance with me
And if the dancing's free,
Then maybe you will have a sweet romance with me!

Life's a waltz, a rumba or a samba,
And you'll feel a whole lot better if you try;
I'd even like to try to dance the mambo -
When I dance I feel that I could touch the sky!

When I dance, I feel your arms around me
And we're whirling with the vigour of the tune
I'm glad you came along and that you found me
When the music stops, it stops an hour too soon!

In the dance then we can feel a little closer
Than when we walk along the terrace or the street
It's one thing here in life that I can go for
Here's a chance for you to sweep me off my feet!

But then dancing's not just made for lovers
And you needn't be committed and in love;
After me then you can dance with many others -
But it won't be me who's giving you the shove!

Hornby Island
1988.07.24

Dreaming
(From "Vancouver Playground")

I dream I've travelled to a hundred suns
In a ship of silver of a million tonnes
Was king of kings and ruled a thousand years
With the power of life and happiness and no more tears.

I dreamed I walked the streets of Samarkand
And found glitt'ring treasures scattered on the sand;
Found sumptuous silks, fine gold and diamonds too,
And when I woke I turned and gave them all to you!

I owned an island in the tropic sun,
Where the beaches sparkled and we lived as one,
The sands were white, the sky was azure blue
And my dreaming wish is that it really all were true!

Chorus: Of all my dreams, those lovely dreams of you
Are those I wish would e'er so quickly all come true!
And all those worlds I visit, I'd deny
If I could wake
and find you lying dreaming by my side!

Hornby Island
1988.07.20

♥

Got to Get Out
(From "Vancouver Playground")

What are you mooning around for?
Why do you gaze at the moon and sigh?
What are you spooning around for,
When you could be a normal and healthy guy?

Chorus: Got to get out and don't be so lazy,
Got to get out and hit the high spots high!
Got to get out and be a little bit crazy,
You gotta be a normal and healthy guy!

Why d'you hold hands in the moonlight,
Wander about like you've lost your way?
Why do you stand in the moonlight?
When you could swing around and you *could* make hay!

Why do you walk by the seashore,
Singing those lovesick and soppy songs?
Got to go raking a bit more -
When you could gaily rattle and bang the gongs!

Why do you sit by the window,
Just waiting for her to come on round?
Soon you'll be ever so thin, you
You gotta try and shake with a joyful sound!

Why don't you go with the gang now?
You're never around when we want some fun.
Let it all go with a bang now!
Come with us - you needn't be the lonesome one!

Vancouver
1988.07.08

✳❤✳

Cuddle Up Close
(From "Vancouver Playground")

I see a star, a-twinkling, oh, so far away,
Its light so distant, yet so clear and bright.
We stop and gaze and wonder at the way
We've come to meet, and feel so close tonight.

Chorus:

Cuddle up close - the night is bright and still.
The days are long when we're far apart.
I hold your hand and all of my senses thrill;
Cuddle up close, and feel my heart.

I feel the breeze a-rippling there upon the pool
Whose surface gleams bright - an enchanted charm.
I draw you close, the night's a little cool
And feel your warmth upon my circling arm.

I hear the sea; its gentle wavelets on the shore,
They ebb and murmur in a silver stream.
The sand is smooth and cooler than before.
We wander on, lost in a magic dream.

I hear the trees so softly sighing over there;
Their feathered tops reach up to touch the moon.
I draw you close, and as I touch your hair,
My heartstrings play a tender, thrilling tune.

Vancouver
1988.07.01

♥

Toodle-ums
(From "Vancouver Playground")

Chorus:
Toodle-ums? Yes, two! Chocolate Toodle-ums? Yes, two!
Don't you think you should have
a chocolate Toodle-um too?

My auntie makes them in her kitchen.
All the best goes in;
Sugar, butter, then some switchin'.
Keeps them in a tin.

I can smell that super savour
From miles away, it seems.
I can taste that super flavour
Even in my dreams!

I can eat them by the dozen,
Any night or day!
I could steal them from my cousin,
Steal them right away!

I can eat them in the bathtub,
Washing off the grime.
I can eat them in the shower,
Or any other time!

I can eat them in the evening,
When all is quiet and still.
I've eaten them since early morning -
And now I'm feeling ill!

West Vancouver
1988.06.28

✳❤✳

The Tea-lady Song
(From "Vancouver Playground")

I'm going to work in a chemist's shop
                  for thirty bucks a day
I'll dish out pills and ointments too,
                  in every kind of way.
But when you've had your fill of pills
                  you'll have to shout for me
Then I'll be around when you feel like a cup of tea!

I'm going to work in a restaurant and get to wait on you.
I'll have to work in the kitchen and
                  I'll wash the dishes too.
And when you're hot and bothered there -
                  that's when I'll heed your plea,
Then I'll be around when you feel like a cup of tea!

I've got a job at the City Hall, it's with the outside crew,
At paving streets and planting trees
                  and laying sidewalks too.
When you're fed up with sweeping streets
                  and take a break at three,
Then I'll be around when you feel like a cup of tea!

I've got a job at the light pipe shop -
                  it's one the college found,
I'll work with bulbs and tubes and things
                  and spread the light around.
When things look black and your bulbs all crack
                  from the electricitee,
Then I'll be around when you feel like a cup of tea!

I'm going to work at pumping gas and I'll be really keen!
I'll polish cars and clear up junk
                  and keep the garage clean.
When you're on the jump at the gasoline pump
                  and wish that you were free,
Then I'll be around when you feel like a cup of tea!

I've got a job as an electrician's mate -
     it's not so swell -
It's with my mother's uncle
     and he'll make me work like hell!
When you're feeling lost and your wires get crossed,
     get down on bended knee -
And I'll be around when you feel like a cup of tea!

I'm going to work at the dancing school,
     where the music's always bright
Teaching rumba, samba, waltz,
     to a new bunch every night.
When your toes get tramped and the guys can't dance
     after lesson fifty-three
Then I'll be around when you feel like a cup of tea!

We've all got jobs in the summertime
     to earn a buck or two,
It gets us all away from Mum and helps our budget too!
It doesn't matter where we work or what our job may be,
We all need a break and a nice hot cup of tea!

      Vancouver
      1988.06.28

I've Got Cramp In My Leg!
(Sung by Louise, in "Vancouver Playground")

I've got cramp in my leg and a chip on my shoulder,
Though I'm so pleasant, that you'd never know!
Watching my friends all get steadily older,
Watching those wrinkles all steadily grow!

It seems only yesterday that I was twenty,
As fair and as free as a song in the air!
Now forty-nine, I've got wrinkles in plenty
And all of my friends know I'm dying my hair!

When I was a girl then I wanted a dream guy,
Tall, handsome and strong - a delight to the eye.
Years passed me by and I found that the real guys
Walked off with my classmates and left me to sigh!

All through my thirties and forties I've waited,
Watched for my dreamy man coming along.
Suddenly, somehow, I think I have found him,
My beautiful daybreak is starting to dawn!

                    Vancouver
                    1988.06.28

＊♥＊

My Pontiac Sixty-two
(From "Vancouver Playground")

Andrew: With my Pontiac 'sixty-two
I've got lots of dirty work to do!
I find I'm out late, by the garden gate,
With my coveralls thick with goo!
And there in the pale moonlight,
I've got to get the brakes just right.
Here's where I have my fun and games -
I don't go out with those flashy dames -
'Cause I've got a date with my old V8 tonight!

Chorus:

A Pontiac 'sixty-two, in nineteen eighty-seven,
Drives away your blues,
and that's my idea of heaven!
Driving around, you feel like a star -
It's just the greatest car!

George: I had a Pontiac 'sixty-two
And I bought it brand spanking new!
Then I was young - now my fling is flung -
According to young folks like you!
But there in the pale moonlight,
(If it's dark then they will not take fright!)
I still enjoy my fun and games
With somewhat older and flashy dames
When I'm out late in my old V8 at night!

Andrew   So here's what you'll have to do
and   With your Pontiac 'sixty-two;
George: Go cruise down the road and take on a load
               Of blondes and a redhead or two!
               And there in the pale moonlight,
               You can cuddle up with all your might;
               There you can have your fun and games,
               There's nothing wrong with those flashy flames,
               When they're out late in your old V8 at night!

Vancouver
1988.06.02

❤

Turn up the Corners
(From "Vancouver Playground")

Worry, worry, worry - always in a hurry!
Why can't I stop, and settle down?
Hustle, hustle, hustle - always in a bustle -
Here and there and out of town!

The answer 's simple - cultivate a dimple
  And smile!

Turn up the corners if you want to relax!
Forget all the phones and the telefax!
Turn up the corners, go swing on a gate!
Turn up that smile and you'll feel just great!

Chorus:
Smile, smile, smile - smile, smile, smile!
Your face won't crack if you try to smile!
A smile's much better than a downcast frown,
So - turn up the corners and smile!

You don't need a palace or a brand-new car
You don't need a bottle at the nearest bar!
Turn up the corners - your face ain't wood!
Turn up the corners and you'll feel so good!

You'll find that smile adds a friendly touch,
So drop that scowl like you'd drop a crutch!
Folks get friendly when they see you smile,
So - turn up the corners and smile!

Go for a wander - take a break from your toil!
A frown's like half a glass of castor oil!
Why not whistle - it's as free as air!
Turn up the corners and smile!

Vancouver
1988.06.13

❃❤❃

Oh, What Joy!

Oh, what joy to see you again!
Oh, what bliss to kiss you again!
To see you now is like sun after rain!
Oh, what joy to hold you again!

My love, your smile is like summer
After a long chilly spell!
I feel like singing,
The church bells are ringing -
I'm laughing and crying as well!

My love, your laugh is like music
Under the silvery moon!
I feel like dancing,
Some solid romancing,
Or singing a welcoming tune!

My love, your touch is like springtime
Caressing the buds on the trees!
I could have told you
How I've longed to hold you
And talk of the birds and the bees.

My love, I hate when you leave me,
The days are so long and so gray,
But when I meet you
And then as I greet you,
My sadness goes whirling away!

Vancouver
1988.05.28

❊❤❊

I See You Standing There
(From "Vancouver Playground")

I see you standing there and my heart stands still;
I run to meet you, dear - all my world's a thrill;
The trees, the flowers and the hedgerows too,
The road, the sky, focus in on you.

Chorus:
I want to sing and dance, I want to laugh and cry,
Your love just fills my heart, so I could touch the sky!
I want to touch the stars, I want to reach the moon,
I want to come to you, I want to hold you soon!

I leave you standing there and it tears my heart,
I long to hold your hand, when we're far apart.
At parting time, then the pain is real,
When you're here again, then it's joy I feel.

Our world is young and fair,
  our love is sweet and true
And life's a joyful song as I cling to you.
This love can never end, this love we feel today,
Sweet love, sweet life, sweet as the flowers in May.

Vancouver
1988.04.10

Patient Relations
(From "Vancouver Playground")

I went to see my quack one day,
Doo-dah, doo-dah
This is what he had to say,
Doo-dah, doo-dah, day.

Chorus:
Go 'n have fun all night;
Go 'n have fun all day;
I'll make you healthy wi' my wee black bag;
Just go and do what I say!

❤

To cure your tennis elbow, dear,
Doo-dah, doo-dah
Drink half pints of lighter beer,
Doo-dah, doo-dah, day.

To preserve your smooth and baby skin
Doo-dah, doo-dah
Cover it well with barrier cream
   and sheets of tin,
Doo-dah, doo-dah, day.

To fix your rotting toenails too,
Doo-dah, doo-dah
Bite them till you're eighty-two
Doo-dah, doo-dah, day.

To stop your hair from turning grey,
Doo-dah, doo-dah
Cut down sex to once a day,
Doo-dah, doo-dah, day.

If you want to hear what people say
Doo-dah, doo-dah
Ask them to repeat it in a friendly way,
Doo-dah, doo-dah, day.

You've got bad cholesterol
Doo-dah, doo-dah
But only in your other ball,
Doo-dah, doo-dah, day.

If you'll do what I tell you to,
Doo-dah, doo-dah
You'll be fit and you can win the Tontine, too,
Doo-dah, doo-dah, day.

Vancouver
1988.04.09

I Scream (Ice Cream!)
(Goes with Clip-clop, lollipop!)
(From "Vancouver Playground")

I scream, I scream - gimme a break!
I'm studying so hard I've got the shakes!
I long for the time, when I've more than a dime
And can buy me a nice piece of steak!

I scream, I scream - gimme a break!
I'm studying so hard I wanna shriek!
I long for the days, when I can just laze
And stay in my bed for a week!

I scream, I scream - gimme a break!
I'm studying so hard I really creak!
I long for the year that I'll wallow in beer
And relax with a book by the creek!

I scream, I scream - gimme a break!
I'm studying so hard I'm just a freak!
I long for that gal, my sweet summer pal,
And to snuggle, caressing her cheek!

I scream, I scream - gimme a break!
I'm so tired now, I cannot stay awake!

Vancouver
1988.03.01

Not Just a Bed of Roses

Many women can't imagine
What it's like to be a man,
To have to shave your chin each morning,
Or stand up to use the can!

Responsibility for family,
Food and welfare as they grow,
Introduces strains and stresses
Many women never know.

Vancouver
1988.03.10

Vancouver Playground
(Sung by George, in "Vancouver Playground")

Though Asia's exotic and has many fans
And Siamese maidens exotic'lly dance
In sinuous loveliness worthy a glance,
I'll always return to Vancouver!

Chorus:

With its long lovely spring
                    and its sweet summer breeze,
Blue sparkling waters, magnificent trees
Bright snow on the mountains, and soft winter rain
There's nowhere that's quite like Vancouver!

Photo: Jim MacCallum

Though English complexions are peaches and crea
(Their summers and winters are never extreme!)
And bonnie Scots lassies were ever my dream,
I'll always return to Vancouver!

Hawaii may beckon with tropical charms;
Grass-skirted beauties with welcoming arms;
And though I may go there again and again,
I'll always return to Vancouver!

I've wandered the world now for many a year,
To the Barrier Reef where I drank Aussie beer,
Saw the girls on the beach in the briefest of gear,
But I'll always return to Vancouver!

Rio, resplendent, in bright blue and green;
Gorgeous mulattoes, the samba school scene;
Though I fell in love with the Carnival Queen,
I'd always return to Vancouver!

Vancouver
1988.03.01

Wonderland
(From "Vancouver Playground")

When you are far away
I miss you every day
Then skies are always gray
I wish you were home!
When you are near to me
You are so dear to me
All things seem clear to me
I'll never roam!

Chorus:

Wonderland, wonderland!
Sweet joy on every hand!
Wearing our wedding bands
Our love will grow!

I want to say to you
I want to stay with you
I want to play with you
Won't that be fun?
Now that you understand
Each time I hold your hand
We're there in Wonderland
Warm in the sun!

Vancouver
1988.02.27

✳❤✳

If You've Been In Love
(From "Vancouver Playground")

Who knows, where my love has gone?
Who knows, lonely hours at dawn?
You ask, do I miss my love?
You'll know, when you've been in love.

Who knows, in the falling rain,
How I seek my love in vain,
And how, in the stars above,
I seek my departed love.

I know, through the passing years
That Time surely dries all tears
And then takes away the pain
And we'll walk with a spring again.

But now - do I miss my love?
You'll know, if you've been in love.

Vancouver
1988.02.22

Delicious Envy

The summer wind caressed your hair,
I've never seen a girl so fair.
    I wish I were the summer wind.

The summer sun that warms your skin
And lights the dimple on your chin -
    I wish I were the summer sun.

The sparkling waves that dance for you
Are objects of my envy too!
    I'd love to be those sparkling waves.

But when you turn and smile at me -
There's no one else I'd rather be!

Vancouver
1988.01.30

Jobs, Jobs, Jobs, Jobs, Jobs
(From "Vancouver Playground")

Chorus(students):

> Jobs, jobs, jobs, jobs, jobs?
> We'd rather be
> Slobs, slobs, slobs, slobs, slobs!
> Who wants it now,
> Work, work, work, work, work?
> We'd rather be
> Jerks, jerks, jerks, jerks, jerks!

(Students)
1.

> We'd rather sit in the sun,
> And be drinkin' our beer,
> Just whilin' the time away.
> But it ain't so much fun,
> We can't buy any gear,
> Without any regular pay!

(Chorus, students):

> (Students)
> And so we come to the school
> Give up most of our time,
> Sit down on those wooden chairs
> And we don't play the fool.
> In the fullness of time,
> We're all goin' to be millionaires!

(Chorus, teachers):
(Teachers)

> Repeat 1.

(Chorus, teachers):

(Teachers)

> And so we come to the school
> For a handful of dirt
> Flaunt professorial airs!
> And recalcitrant fools
> We all strive to convert
> To tractable, sweet, millionaires!

(Chorus, all)

> Vancouver
> 1988.02.22

✳❤✳

Tennis Party,
St Abbs,
1930

Left to right: Duncan

Back row:	?	?	?	MacCallum
Front row:	Alex	Sadie			Jack
	Nisbet	McGhie	?	?	MacCallum

Nameless Photographs

The faces in the photographs look out at us today
From picnics, outings, holidays, of very long ago.
We can almost hear their voices,
             sense their fun and laughter, gay;
There are one or two we recognize,
             but most we'll never know.
There's Mum and Dad in '32,
             in black and white and gray,
With Mother in a tennis dress, or Grandpa with a hoe.
Uncle Nicol, cousin Jean, another child at play,
With bucket, spade, his eyes in shade,
             just gazing at his toe!

Going back just ten more years - it's not so easy then -
Two couples on a bench, just lounging -
             others playing games.
Some just might be aunts we knew -
             but who are all the men?
Moustached and whiskered, sunburned, pale
             - is that one maybe James?
There's no one left to answer all the questions that we pen;
We know that we're related,
             but we'll never know their names.

                       Montreal, 1988.01.11

❤

We're Going To A Wedding
(From "Vancouver Playground")

Chorus:
We're going to a wedding
A glorious wedding
We're going to a wedding
The likes of which has never been seen before.

(By Andrew:)   There'll be Pappa and Mamma and Sally and Jim
All waiting by the aisle
And though I'll be nervous, I'll give you a smile
Full of my love to the brim!

(Chorus)

(By Mary-Ann:)   Our friends will be waiting with boisterous cheers
And all dressed up so fine
And think of those kisses, those kisses like wine,
We'll share on down through the years!

(By father:)   I'll get dressed up in my swallow-tail coat
For cheering on the bride.
Her joyfulness makes me so happy inside
And gives me a lump in my throat.

(Chorus)

(By George:)   There'll be speeches and singing and maybe a tear
And much good food so swell
There'll be whisky and soda and champagne as well
But just lead me on to the beer!

(Chorus)

(By Louise:)   I'll be painted and scented and waving a fan
To match my elegant gown.
I'll be smiling and laughing, with never a frown -
And maybe then I'll get that man!

(Chorus)

West Vancouver
1988.01.11

✳♥✳

Dentists and Things

If a crown comes loose
when you're chewing a piece of moose
You'll have to see a dentist
and he'll pluck you like a goose
They have the best receptionists, the best of everything
And make a lot more money than the king!

A real palaeontologist struts his stuff in caves.
They also have a lot of fun
when scratching round in graves;
Their homes are full of bones and rocks
and artifacts on shelves
But some of them are dinosaurs themselves!

You can be an electrician
and deal with wires and things.
You have to know your volts and amps
and how a buzzer rings.
It sounds a little dull to me, but then, it's hard to tell
'Cause *they* do lots of shocking things as well!

West Vancouver
1988.

✻❤✻

A Maudlin Memory Of Robert Burns

I staggered round in Mauchline town
And in the churchyard sought a stone
On which to sit and slowly think -
My thoughts befuddled wi' the drink
And perchance to deeply ponder
Life's true meaning. Over yonder
In the pub, I heard, I thought,
Them mutter, darkly, "Stone the sot!"

But what care I for criticism?
Life is but a witticism!
A chance to dally wi' the lasses!
I view the world through rosy glasses!

And then I heard an angel sing,
Clear and pure - and then I groaned,
The message was - "The sot is stoned!"

West Vancouver
1988.01.12

Car pool Capers
(From "Vancouver Playground")

We organize the car pools here for all the student crew
We sympathize, we empathize,
try not to make you blue!
We shuffle and we shift around the combinations rare
Until we get a match for you!

It's not a job that's easy 'cause they're such a picky bunch!
They come to us at ten o'clock
and want it fixed by lunch!
Their wants are sometimes crazy and they make us tear our hair
Until we get a match for you!

We had a girl who came to us and asked us what to do.
She couldn't stand the smell of men,
smoke and garlic too!
We found the only answer was a gas mask, so you see,
We're sure to find a match for you!

And then there was the Scotsman with his kilt and hairy knees;
He liked to sit upon the roof
so he could feel the breeze!
He lasted just about a week - we think he blew away!
We'll get a better match for you!

Once we had a Chinese girl who wore a Chinese frock.
We sent her on her way at once -
she said she liked to walk!
We realized, long after that, a wok's for Chinese food!
We'll get a better match for you!

Computers now can pair you off in each and every way,
Accommodate each preference
in all your work and play.
We are not responsible if you should fall in love
Although we made the match for you!

West Vancouver
1988.01.12

✳♥✳

A Family Christmas

The lighted candles on the wall
The shouts and laughter in the hall
Where Mum and Dad greet one and all
To a family Christmas.

The crackling fire, the sparkling tree,
The smallest child on Grandpa's knee,
Excited eyes, so wide to see
A special family Christmas.

You feel excitement building up
As more arrive and take the cup
Of warm good cheer that stirs the pulse
Of a family Christmas.

The friendly toast to "Absent Friends"
Caresses memories and sends
Our thoughts a-winging o'er the years
To an earlier Christmas.

The uncles then had different names -
Pete and Guy, not Mike and James.
The children too, played different games
In an earlier Christmas.

Warming dishes and platters too,
Warmer glances from me to you,
Putting together our version, it's true,
Of that family Christmas.

Coloured paper, tinsel, string,
All who want are free to sing,
Songs rehearsed, or freely given,
To make a family Christmas.

♥

When all have gone, we close the door,
The kids in bed, there are thoughts galore,
Of other times and other places,
Other people, other faces.
A little different, yet the same,
The same old family Christmas.

West Vancouver
1987.12.24

Muddled Midnight Meanderings

Awake, one day, in the night there's a sound
Of wind from afar, not the wind from a car
With tyres that squeal, but rather a har-
dly digested meal!
It may not have been a fart from a bean,
But, rather, a fart from a fresh butter tart!
When I say a tart, I don't mean a bird,
But, rather, a tart that was baked by a bird!
Not a bird on the wing, but a bird in the hand
(Worth two in the bush - or beats the band)!

This may be confused, but you'll soon understand.
Understanding is simple, this poem of a bird -
But the poem's not simple - just simply absurd!

West Vancouver
1987.11.06

❋♥❋

The Vancouver Smoker's Consolation

This is a nuclear and smoke-free zone
Where the air is ever so clean
So please don't impart
E'en a delicate fart
Or you'll sully the corporate scene!

As you all are aware, both the halls and the stair
In the office are fed from one fan,
So the gas you exude
From your Indian food
Could screw up the overall plan.
(What becomes of the smells from the can?)

Onions are out, and so is spiced trout,
Garlic and sumptuous curry;
And menthol gum
Would be horrible, chum,
Although you may chew in a hurry!

So - smokers, beware, as you contemplate there,
To quit smoking just isn't enough -
It's equally easy
To make us all queasy
By using alternative stuff!

The message is clear, just the whiff of a beer
Would be shared by us all in a flash.
Yield not to Temptation! Your one consolation -
We ALL have to cancel our lunchtime libation -
As you think of your fags in the trash!

West Vancouver
1987.01.25

❋❤❋

Those Golden Ears

"People note a hearing loss
Much more than a hearing aid."
I didn't make this up myself -
That's what the brochure said!

It may be true, but it seems to me
It's salesmanship, transparent
And a lost hearing aid at five hundred bucks
Is a damn sight more apparent!

West Vancouver
1987.01.25

To Rick Morrit - the Hornby Island Plumber -
Now Even My Conscience is Clean!

When I didn't send the cash
It was an oversight;
Not that I didn't mean to pay
Your billing, out of spite!
It may appear that I have waited
Just to hear you holler
That you're watching both the cents
And each delightful dollar!

I knew at once that you must have
Scots blood in your veins,
Counting both the precious pounds
And the priceless pence!

With conscience clear, now I am humming,
Every time I use your plumbing!

West Vancouver
1987.07.10

✳❤✳

Going, Going...... Gone?

Another old lady's candle is guttering;
Sarah, then Daisy, now Florence, it seems.
Funny - I notice my own heartbeat fluttering -
Maybe it signals the end of my dreams?

I'd like to publish the poems that I'm writing,
Pass on my thoughts to my children, one day.
The thought of extinction is none too inviting -
It's hard to write limericks, cold in the clay!

    I'd like to go round again,
    If I could just now and then
    Hold hands with my darling Jane
    And wander some sunset beach
    And fondle her skin, like peach.
    Or will it be out of reach?

        West Vancouver
        1987.06.22

Fireflies

    I saw the fireflies by the road,
    One evening in Buckingham,
    Dancing, winking,
    Swooping, blinking
    'twas fascinating how they glowed.

    The grass was gently tinted green,
    The stars were showing, faintly,
    Day declining,
    Distant shining
    Lights to guide a fairy queen.

It's strange how their phenomenon
Seems to be more permanent;
Everlasting,
Quite contrasting
Our short flick'ring, quickly gone.
They'll be here, every year,
Like the sun, when we're done!

But - a spark of us persists
Through our children, down the mists!

Buckingham, Quebec
1987.06.22

"Gather Ye Rosebuds..."

I watched a lovely butterfly
Flutter by a leafy tree,
Aware of me,
Seeing something I can't see.

Maybe it was just romancing.
Leaves a-dancing, brightly gay,
Did they say
To the butterfly that day

"Dance and flutter - gather hay!
Winter's winds come after May!
Dance and flutter - honeymoon!
There won't be another June!"?

Too soon come Winter's desolations
Replacing Summer's sweet sensations.

West Vancouver
1987.06.22

Eighty Years - A Wink

I watched you, Mother, young and fair,
Maybe pastry in your hair,
Cutting veg. or stirring soup,
Charming cakes from sticky goop!

Handing you the clothespegs
In the chilly, sunny blast,
I hear the blankets flapping
In a sunny childhood past.

The many children playing
in the rowdy, darkened hall;
You dozing in a comfy chair,
oblivious to all!

Much later then, I'd take you home,
up to the second floor,
And then we'd hug goodbye beside
the elevator door.

Christmas, happy, tears of joy,
then ten days farther on
I saw your eyelids flicker
and I knew that you were gone.

The world will be a harder place
Without your gentle, loving face.

West Vancouver
1987.01.28

✳❤✳

When I Cry

I still can't believe that my Mummy has gone,
I watched as she just ebbed away.
My sadness is deep as the still boundless ocean
Where billows and memories play.

She sat by the seashore when I was a boy,
Laughing and smiling with me.
I walk by the seashore and still hear the waves,
But all that is left is the sea.

She joyed in the contact with all of her children,
Her gladness apparent to all whom she knew,
She aye made the best of each lingering moment
And always let joyous things lighten her view.

I long for your smiling eye
To comfort me, when I cry.

West Vancouver
1987.01.28

Photo: Jim MacCallum

✳❤✳

Trivial Pursuits

I wake up in the dead of night
Comfy, warm and cosy.
My wife lies there, insensible,
Cheeks all red and rosy.

I lie awhile, get up to pee,
Have a little drink,
Water only - I must add
- and then I start to think
Of all the things I have to do,
All the bills to pay,
All the things I should have done
And didn't, yesterday!

Those trivial thoughts go trundling on
And with them, slowly, comes the dawn!

West Vancouver
1986.12.19

✳❤✳

Nightmare and Consolation

When you wake at night
In a blinding fright,
Sweating from every pore,
With the house on fire
Like a funeral pyre
And a demon denying the door!

A nameless dread,
A talking head,
An AIDS-ridden glass-eyed whore,
A corpse that looks like Uncle Fred
- Terrible things, and more!

Drowning in crud, fields of blood,
Machine-guns, minefields and gore;
Burning grain, a child in pain,
An animal caught in a snare.
To awake from alarms
To two loving arms,
Is relief, beyond compare!

West Vancouver
1986.12.16

One Way Out

To watch one's mother slowly die
- All her friends are gone -
Is sadness, heartbreak, stifled tears
And feet just dragging on.

She'd never ever take a pill
And choose the easy way -
"You never want to just give in."
Is what I've heard her say!

I run to catch a traffic light,
Run upstairs a bit
I'd rather have a heart attack
Than moulder here in shit!

I realise that an early death
Won't win the Tontine jackpot,
But rather dead, a happy corpse
Than a rich and dribbling crackpot!

West Vancouver
1986.12.16

✳❤✳

That Time of the Month

My cheque went NSF today
And brought that sinking feeling!
Each time it happens, I believe
It's character-revealing!

I do my job most carefully,
Cross my "t"s and dot my "i"s,
But when it comes to money
Then I'm hardly money-wise!

I lack financial planning -
It's decidedly unmanning!
I must be doing something wrong
- Each month's at least a week too long!

And running out of money
Isn't fucking funny!

West Vancouver
1986.12.14

❋♥❋

Short and Sweet

Clip-clop,
Lollipop;
White van,
Nice man;
Seven cents,
Heaven-sent!
Kid's dream,
Ice cream!

West Vancouver
1986.12.12

I Can't Stop Loving You

"I can't stop loving you"
I wish were my line!
I'd change the sentiment
- Get rid of the whine!

"I can't help wanting you"
I'm happy to say!
I'll spend my whole life through, with you,
In love-inspired play!

West Vancouver
1986.12.13

Photo: Jim MacCallum

Once Upon A Time

Remember crawling through the leaves,
Their touch, their sound, their smell?
Remember racing round the park
And "chases" by the well?
Kick-the-can and hide-and-seek,
Cops and robbers too;
It seems like yesterday to me
And much the same to you!

We climbed the hills to see the view,
We tumbled through the greens,
We raced along the tops of walls,
And squabbled with our frien's.
We picnicked with the Sunday School,
Tramcarred to the Zoo.
I haven't changed a bit inside
- But neither then, have you!

How can it be that Yesterday
- so bright, so clear - so far, so near -
Can suddenly be "Once upon a time"?

West Vancouver
1986.12.12

✻♥✻

My Love

I see your eyes in dreams so fair,
Your lovely arms, your lips, your hair,
I only wish that I were there,
Entwined in loving passion.
When I come home, come up the stair,
You're on the landing, waiting there,
Always neat, and dressed with flair,
Yet not a slave to Fashion.

Your hands are strong, and shapely too,
Your touch is soft, forever new,
I catch your eye at every chance;
Do others see our secret glance?
Or see my touch as I pass your chair,
Or feel the love as I touch your hair?

West Vancouver
1986.07.03

Dave Turnbull

I know a little barmaid,
Buxom, blonde and boozy;
I watch her every evening long
And feel like breaking into song
- She makes my knees quite woozy!

I paint and recite impeccably,
I'm good at my job - kontrolls;
I luv my bote, I'm at home aflote,
However she pitches and roles.

I'm a simpel man with simpel taists,
But my spelling would maik you wince.
I came from the womb relucktantlee
- 've been trying to get back ever since!

West Vancouver
1986.07

✳❤✳

Insomnia

When I can't sleep,
I don't count sheep,
I'll pen a little ditty.
The rhyming words come thick and fast,
Pity, pretty, shitty!

West Vancouver
1986.07.04

The Competitor

I wear my little hat these days
to keep me from the cold;
Not because - whate'er you think -
because I'm growing old!
Sex in moderation,
Lots of contemplation
On how I'll go, in a white hot glow,
If only I can stick around
With both my feet above the ground,
As all the years unfold.

I'd like to say I'm training hard,
but then, that's hardly true;
I'm just another veg'table -
a lump of Scottish stew!
I've got the Tontine round my neck,
Becoming quite a nervous wreck,
Lying awake at night and thinking,
cogitating too,
On ways and means to win the race,
Get fitter, faster, and avoid
Being beat by one of you!

West Vancouver
1986.07

❤

Halley - in Eastern Transvaal

A swallow swoops and scintillates
in copper-burnished blue.
The garden's glades are deep in shade,
The hills are drenched in sun,
While 'scarpments grand, on every hand,
Like rosy walls of Samarkand,
Look down, unseeing, too.

A pigeon coos, then arcs across
the froth-bedappled sky,
While, by the pool, the children fool,
So careless, every one.
Their lives are fleet as nimble feet
And, doubtless, almost all complete,
As will be you and I.

The battlemented mountains, though,
Will feel the comet's ghostly glow.

Watervaal Boven
1986.04.06

❤

The Big Five Oh

How can I ignore the flow
Of all the years that swiftly go,
My childhood seems so long ago;
I have reached the big Five Oh!

I can still remember when
A sack of coal cost two-and-ten;
Now all the boys I knew are men.
I have reached the big Five Oh!

I watch the money rolling in,
I guess I'd rather roll in Sin,
But my chances now are very thin,
Now I've reached the big Five Oh!

I'm in a pretty leaky boat,
Old Father Time's begun to gloat,
Reincarnation's got my vote,
Now I've reached the big Five Oh!

My eyes are quickly growing dim,
My hair is fast becoming thin
But, worst, my little brother, Jim
Soon will reach the big Five Oh!

Eight-oh, seven-oh, six-oh, five-oh -
Just be glad that you're alive-oh!

West Vancouver
1985.12.15 (The Big Five-oh!)

Nightmare

Got some work done, read some notes, had a little nap;
Sat there quietly dosing, with my hands upon my lap;
Had some dinner, chicken breast, sipped a pleasant wine,
Liqueur and coffee, dreamed of you, arrival half-past-nine.

Sudden shudder! What the hell...? Consternation reigns;
All awake and staring, wondering, listening, stomach pains.
       "We seem to have a problem.."
       - the voice is tense and clear.
On every face is written terror, apprehension, fear.

       My boys, my love I'll never see,
       A note she'll never read.
       I never should have travelled.
       My heart begins to bleed.

S.O.S.; Mayday, Mayday, Mayday; help, help, help;
Dit-dit-dit; dah dah dah; dit-dit-dit;
Holy shit; falling, tumbling, far; this is IT!

       Blackness - dark and all-embracing -
       Loving, laughter, life, effacing.

       Ottawa
       1985.08.21

✳❤✳

Rush, Rush, Rush!

I have a very beautiful wife
With a loving smile and a warm embrace.
My only regret is that this short life
Goes hurrying on with relentless pace.

Tokyo, Medan and Singapore,
New Orleans, Meridian, Santiago and more;

All in a lonely blur.

Medan
1985.05

Fujiyama Train - of Thought

Fuji in cloud is majestic, serene,
Mist-edged and silent.
The children are boisterous, laughing and clean,
Lively and vibrant.

The cone unattainable, 'minds me of Love's
Memory, haunting;
My love's distant beauties, like-shrouded in dreams,
Love all enchanting.

Sleep, work and dreamlessness, haste time away
And numb recollection
Of hours in your arms, breathing deep of your warm
And loving perfection.

I ache for you, my love; my dreams
Are just frustration's goad, it seems!

Tokyo
1985.05.29

Tontine Tonterias

If I should win the Tontine
I would wallow deep in cash;
Spend a bit, donate a bit,
           or purchase something rash!

I haven't stopped to calculate
         the sum that may accrue,
But I would hope I'd have the scope
To wash with honey-scented soap
- Instead of Rickett's Blue!

I'd buy a brand-new motor car
- No longer would I need
To save my pennies in a jar.
And when I feel just under par
I'd fly to islands drenched in sun,
Drink martinis by the jug,
         eat truffles by the ton!

But - one dark shadow rears its head -
Ten special friends would all be dead
- Not to name my Mum!

Well - you can shove that little lot
- I'm happy with the friends I've got
- Though they're somewhat polyglot!

This change of heart may well have caused
No little consternation,
But you'll agree with me, I think,
There's little consolation
In having all that dough to spend
In splendid isolation!

                  West Vancouver
                  1984.11.22

✳❤✳

Chile, in Memory

Santiago's pollution's a desperate sea
Of buses, noise, smoke like perdition;
People, paseos, the six o'clock crush,
Hawkers in hot competition.

A mother and child on the steps of a church
Pleading a pitiful peso,
As couples go by in a world all alone,
Loving glances and intimate beso.

Clustering shacks on the crest of a hill,
A cross, broken streets and a river;
But a black-haired and laughing and chattering child
Is the Chile remembered forever.

Santiago de Chile
1984.08

To You, My Woman

The sea is living silver
In the late Chilean rays.
But there's a sadness in the sundown
Of these lingering, fleeting days.

There is only one life.
Yes, that's what I believe,
First, songs and joy and laughter,
Then we gradually grieve.

My only real life is in your loving arms,
Then I live and love and feel
The warmth of your affection;
Life's a jewel, loving, real.

When I travel, I am cheated;
Precious moments just unreel.

Constitucion, Chile
1984.08

✳❤✳

Going Crazy

Oh, I love you in the evening when the light is growing dim
Or the morning when the sky is eggshell blue.
If the day were any longer I would die of growing fonder
For I find I'm growing crazy over you.

The first time that I saw you, it must have been your eyes
That made me want to come and talk with you.
That simple first attraction was translated into action
And I started going crazy over you.

We chatted and we had such fun and wandered through the town,
Hand-in-hand, just as growing lovers do.
In the shadow of the trees I'd be down on bended knees
Which were weak from being crazy over you.

West Vancouver
1984.05

A Card for Mum

Happy Birthday, Eighty!
I'm glad you're not as weighty
As your "little" sister!
And may all the exercise
Keep you happy, healthy, wise!

Vancouver
1984.05.22(written on 21st)

✳❤✳

Pre-operational Trauma

Dark imaginings prolong the waking,
Yet we hurtle, unchecked, towards the dawn.
"Will the knife work? Will my wife walk?
Are but two of the questions that yawn.

The answers - a litany - dark as the night,
Are leaden, as heavy as Time
That crushes us, changes us, grinds us to husks
From the children we were - for a time.

The aches and the stiffness, the slackness of skin,
All tell us that Youth is forbye;
Our lives are so fleet - in the morning, at ten,
We may just look Death in the eye.

My love, my love - you ask, will I wait?
We'll lovingly go, hand in hand, to the gate.

West Vancouver
1984.03.04

❄❤❄

Hostile Hotels

I'm lying in limbo, the darkness surrounds;
My regular breathing, the solit'ry sound.
The bedroom is alien and I don't belong.
To lie here without you just has to be wrong.
In lonely hotel rooms, the loneliness broods
            And nurtures my longing.

I try to imagine your face and your smile,
I look at your picture and ponder awhile
On the pleasures of travel, the shortness of life
And desp'rately missing my sweet loving wife,
Who's sure I'm out raking and painting the town
            - Can't imagine my longing.

And close in the darkness the worsening pain
Of the nights and the miles till I see you again.

1984.01

An Observation

You know times are really tough
When sonnets only have twelve lines!

West Vancouver
1984.01

❤ *Valentine 1984* ❤

The beach, the trees, the summer breeze,
Your laugh, your smile, your shapely knees,
The waves, the sky, your beckoning eye
and don't forget, your apple pie,
All combine in a dream sublime
- Please won't you be my Valentine?

West Vancouver
1984.02

✳❤✳

Night Sounds

The night is quiet, I hear a train,
Muffled, down the hill.
A car goes by, a sudden noise,
But otherwise, it's still.
Every other tiny sound is magnified, and clear
(especially the high-pitched hum
That's always in my ear!).

The sounds I miss are little ones
- Your quiet breathing, there -
I miss the subtle fragrance
In your pillow, of your hair.
The curtain breathes, accentuates
The stillness all around
- I'm sure I'd hear a leaflet, soundless,
Thudding to the ground.

But to hear you turning towards me
With a sleepy sigh, a smile,
Would be worth a mighty pilgrimage,
A hundred thousand mile.

1983.08.19

Sweet Insomnia

Too wide awake to fall asleep,
Too sleepy, though, to   read;
It's kind of nice to be awake
With lovely, lively, you.

West Vancouver
1983.02

❤

Svensk Baksmälla!

Fy katten, jag har ondt i skallen,
Världen gupper upp och ned;
Spriten som jag tog har gjort
Att horisonten ligger sned!

or - in English -

Swedish Hangover!

By jings, I've got a splitting headache,
The world is bouncing like a clown;
The demon drink I took prevents
The damn horizon lying down!

1982.08.29

Brasilian Dreaming

I sit and while away the flight,
Or lie and dream away the night,
Seeing you at home.
I see you in the kitchen,
Or sorting out some stitching,
Or chatting on the phone.

I see you in a pretty dress
Or cursing at the children's mess,
As though they were your own!
I see you wear this cotton dress
And see its gentle folds caress
You, lovely as a poem.

I see you in the bedroom, dear,
With breasts so full, eyes shining, clear,
And love just you alone.

1982.04

❉❤❉

Lonely in South Africa

I lie and hug my pillow
And dream that pillow's you,
- But I'll have to wait another week
Before that dream comes true!

N'godwana
1982.05

Happy-ever-after-o

Oh ho-ro, my nut-brown maid,
Along the beaches, through the glade,
A lovely dance 't is we have led
    Along the ways, together-o.

Sunshine-dappled nose and chin,
Sparkling eyes and golden skin,
Our thought and hearts are close akin,
    Just wandering, together-o.

And when winter's icy chill
Bares the birches on the hill,
My thoughts fly on to where they will
    To summertime, together-o.

When the summer comes again,
We will wander to the glen
An frolic in the waves again,
    So happily, together-o.

Oh, I love thee, nut-brown maid,
Along the beaches, through the glade,
A lovely dance 't is we have led,
    Along the ways, together-o.

West Vancouver
1981.11

❤

The Wanderer's Premature Return

I can't sleep, can't eat and I wander
All around the room.
The clock strikes three, or maybe half-past two.
I've had my fill of looking around
And seeing a sight or two
And I can't stay
     Another day away
         from you!

I've got backache, heartache, and I'm needing
Loving through and through.
I miss my bed, but most I'm missing you.
So I'm flying home, two whole days early
Via Honolu' -
Just couldn't stay
     Another day away
         from you!

There's a creamtime, dreamtime, coming soon,
It's absolutely true!
The clouds slip by below me, tinged with blue.
Nine hundred kilometres nearer, darling,
Every single hour -
I won't have to stay
     Another day away
         from you!

           Over the Pacific
           1981.10.16

❇❤❇

Awakening

I wandered through a dream of gold
In a land where it was never cold
And where the sea was always crystal blue.

The sand was white as polished bone,
The trees were a green I'd never known
And seemed to reach to touch the azure sky.

The people there were strong and bold
And showed no signs of growing old.
Their skin was bronzed a lovely golden hue.

And you were there beneath the trees,
Your hair was rippling in the breeze,
But you were kissing someone else,
                and made me cry.

West Vancouver
1981.10.04

A Lover Like You

You are my love, Jane -
But won't believe
It and, in vain, you lie and grieve.

I want your lips,
Your eyes, your smile;
You think I'll ditch you
And revile
Me, your love, from time to time.
It's nuts when love is so sublime!

Don't you worry, sweet, my pet -
Up till now, I've never met
A lover quite like you!

Buenos Aires
1981.06.19

❤

Hope Doesn't Spring Eternal

They sit and dream
The food grows cold,
One sees they know
They're growing old.

The man they're with has lost his charm,
They'd love to feel another arm,
At least, to me, today, it seems,
To realize their wildest dreams.

Their eyes are empty,
Words are few.
The evening drags,
And loving, too.
What luck *we* have -
Just me and you!

La Estancia, Buenos Aires
1981.06.19

Shooting Star

The people in Nanaimo saw
The Northern Lights above -
But it was only Colin and Jane
On Hornby - making love!

West Vancouver
1980.07.20

Just Think

I might get a trip to Gothenburg soon
And I'd go via Glasgow and Oslo;
I'd visit relations and many a friend,
I'd see many places I'd love to again.

Hyndland and Partick would give me a glow;
Dally in Dalsholm, walk Campsie Glen;
Tarry in London and go to a show,
See Piccadilly, the river, Big Ben.

Janne and Ingemar, Aunt Daisy and Babs;
I'd see Jimmy's kids, though they've grown;
Wander in Oslo in Vigeland Park
And surely have coffee with Kari.

The pictures are colourful, clear and profuse
And the wanting is sharp and familiar.

Many have wandered - and many are dead
And even the places have changed -
There are bridges, and highways, and houses anew,
And I, as a visitor - changed a bit, too.

West Vancouver
1980.05.08

Photo: Jim MacCallum

✳❤✳

AC619-421-149 Halifax-Montreal-Toronto-Vancouver*

I'd love to fly to Glasgow
And see my people there -
Aunt Nancy, Averill, Daisy
And there are mony mair;
I'd love to see the Kelvin
And the bonny brae behind,
Where I wandered wi' my Mairi
On mony a grassy wynd.

We're all a whole lot older
And our fathers passed away,
But the memories are fresh and green,
They could be yesterday.
I'm sitting in a 747 and chase the dying day,
Leaving Nova Scotia -
       and <u>Old</u> Glasgow's far away.

West Vancouver
1980.05.08

Still Awake

I've been awake since five past two
Thinking constantly of you.
All fired up now the chips are down,
I'm just the happiest guy in town.

Thinking of the summer in a cottage with you,
Thinking of the swimming - and the cuddling too!
Hoping in the darkness that my writing can be read,
Longing just to hold you in a lovely warm bed!

West Vancouver
1980.01.10

✳❤✳

❤ *Valentine's Day, 1980* ❤

Upside down and round about,
Love's as sweet as wine;
So, in this topsy-turvy world,
Please be my Valentine!

———

Here's a little pussy -
I wish that he were thine,
She brings a thought from me to thee -
Please be my Valentine!

———

Here we are at Valentine's
- No fun to be away -
But be patient and you'll get
  A kiss another day.

———

I have to say that torrid nights
Are just my cup of tea.
I wouldn't mind another cup
- Love to you from me.

———

❤

It's Early, Love - or Early Love

I wake in the night and the hours slip by -
It's going on four and I wakened at two.
My arms are so empty, my heart is so full,
My old life's in tatters, I'm longing for you.

I think of the children, they'll manage, I'm sure;
They're young and they love us, respectively too,
Our lives are our own, and this feeling's so pure,
We've love and to spare for those kids, me and you.

It's warm in the darkness, the night is so still,
The snow on the sidewalk is six inches deep.
This loving, this rapture's a glorious thrill,
It isn't a wonder we're both lacking sleep.

I'll see you today and we'll ski and we'll hug,
And we'll scheme
        and we'll chatter, two bugs in a rug.

West Vancouver
1980.01.10

Aluminum City Housekeeping Unit

May I extend a fond hello
From somewhere nearing ten below,
Fahrenheit - what a night!

Bed's too short, feet are cold,
Bathroom's sporting bright green mould.
Sheer disgrace - what a place!

But I'm grateful in this frozen dormer
For dreams of you that make it warmer.
Thoughts a-whirl - what a girl!

I haven't known you fifteen hours,
So why's the world all strewn with flowers?
Double ration - mutual passion!

Sleep.

Kitimat, 1980.01.08

The Kitimat Road

The mountains glow pink in the morning sun,
The sky is an eggshell blue,
The Kitimat road is ahead and I'd love
To be sharing the journey with you.

There's a cloud on the crest
 of the steep wooded hill
Like a pillar of white hot fire.
The frost swirls white in a withering wind
Over the road and the hard-frozen mire.

A sudden bright flash as the sun strikes the car
And lights up the forest around.
A small flock of songbirds soars in the sky,
Flashes past, but I can't hear their sound.

Sharp scarlet girders and bright greeny rails
Span the silver-blue streak of the stream.
Bare boulders border the banks, and the ice
Is ink-black and dotted with cream.

The Kitimat vista then stretches away
- I wish we had seen it together, today.

Kitimat
1980.01.08

Sunset from WA760 - 3 October 1979

I never saw a sunset like the one I saw today,
Climbing from the fogginess of indistinct L.A.;
The reds and yellows, blues and greys,
                and purples in between,
Just had to be the finest sight that I have ever seen.

It took just moments, not much more,
            to reach the clouds above
And left a pleasant memory
            like consummated love.

Los Angeles, 1979.10.03

Haakon

Haakon, running at three or four,
Long slim feet barely touching the floor
In total racing abandon.
Eyes just full of excited joy,
Eagerly seeking a mischievous ploy
Or a bed or a sofa to land on.

Trousers flapping at ankles and knees,
Loose-limbed and light as a warm summer breeze,
Always so happy and willing to please.

Triangular nails and a flat big toe
Sticking up at an angle. Eyes shine, clear, below
A tall, narrow forehead, and fringe.
        Always raring to go -
        Action, action, action!

Loving and welcoming, happy to greet
Mummy or Daddy, however dead beat.
You feel it's so genuine, so naive and so warm,
This little boy's loving and welcoming charm.

                    West Vancouver
                    1978.10.01

✻❤✻

Invitation

Would you like a walk in the snow, my love,
In the clear dark night 'neath the moon, my love,
Just you and me, all alone, my love
- Are you tempted? Come!

The crunch of the snow underfoot, my love,
The trees' white tracery arching above,
A touch, or a kiss of blossoming love
Would be lovely. Come!

West Vancouver
1978.01.09

Anticipation

The thought of seeing my lover, this evening, for a while
Just fills my being with delight and love.
I feel my heartbeat quicken, in good old-fashioned style
And sense her love around me, like a glove.
My blood goes flowing quickly through
my veins, my fingers tingle
I could not bear the thought of you
and I being once more single.
The thought of seeing my lover
sets heart and cheek a-glow,
The glowing warmth of love's sweet fireside ingle.

West Vancouver
1977.10.09

No Strings?

As we near the end of summer, Jane,
One thing you ought to know -
If you'll be my second fiddle, then
I'll gladly be your beau!

Davis Bay
1977.07.22

✳❤✳

May-to-September 1977

We shared so many summer sunsets,
Walked so many stony strands,
Saw so many swooping seabirds,
Raced along the Welcome sands.

We swam down through the cool green water,
Saw the flash of arm and thigh,
Saw the sparkling drops enhancing
Sunburned face and smiling eye.

Too quickly summer evenings shorten
And summer sunsets loose their glow -
More quickly now than I remember,
As we approach this year's September.

> Davis Bay
> 1977.07.17

Holidays - 1977

The peace and quiet of Davis Bay
Are only twenty miles away,
But could be on the moon!

The trouble with my holidays
- Just like the Nova's super blaze -
They're over far too soon!

> Davis Bay
> 1977.07.15

✳❤✳

Revelation

Just as I woke this morning
A thought rushed into my mind,
Not a lightning flash or a thunderclap
Even worse than that - I miss you.

West Vancouver
1977.04

Jane

I view your green eyes with delight
And see that smile, your lips transforming;
I see them in the darkest night
- and fear they may be habit-forming.

And in your figure, lissom there,
A woman's loveliness abiding;
I see your hair all shot with grey,
A broad and lovely forehead hiding.

I'd love to spend more time with you
And know how loneliness distresses -
It also gives more value to
Your loving glance and fond caresses.

West Vancouver
1977.04

✳❤✳

Some Feelings

I don't know, Jane, why I'm writing this,
But there's a glow and a wanting inside
      that I can't identify.
It isn't love, but I see your eyes
In the semi-darkness - and long to see them again.

I can smell your scent in the dynetrekk,
I can feel the touch of your hair on my cheek
And hear your voice, insistently, softly,
      longingly saying "Colin, Colin",
And again, in the semi-darkness - I long to hear it again.

There's warmth and newness in the way we hold hands,
There's that pit-of-the-stomach feeling
      that I thought was gone,
But our lives are so complex, and their webs
      so intricately spun,
That only in the semi-darkness, with you,
      do I know which way to turn.

If life were only loving, perhaps it would be easier;
If we could drown in the pool of a longing gaze
And never have to come up for air in the world of reality,
Living always in a warm and loving embrace.

                  Chicago-Seattle, NW27
                  1977.04.06

✳❤✳

Cold Comfort

There's no horizon and the grey sky merges
With the greying distant whiteness of the snow.
The wind sweeps blindly o'er the runway verges
Where the taxiing lights all blue and dimly glow.

The snow makes patterns on the grim black tarmac,
The formations change as soundlessly they flow
In first one direction, then they turn back
In a freezing dance at twenty-four below.

That's Winnipeg with winter chills
- In Vancouver there are daffodils!

Winnipeg
1977.02.02

Wrong Train - Again!

Riding down to Bangor,
On an eastern train -
It should have been to Gretna Green -
I've done it wrong again!

Vancouver
1977.01.20

Edmonton Sunset

Flat snowy fields and a vast sky,
Toothbrush clumps of trees - now - don't ask why -
Rosy clouds and grey wisps all fly high.

Zenith blue, blue-grey, duck-egg blue,
Glowing purple grey and an orange hue,
Blinding yellow sun saying goodbye to you.

Little lights now sparkle on the skyline there,
The yellow blaze is orange, unsurpassing fair,
The sun becomes a molten reddish flare.

The blue fades to dove grey, the dark is near.
Shadows blacken, indistinct, some stars appear:
The western skyline's mountains stand there,
                              sharp and clear.

A crimson ribbon, streaked with black, the day is gone,
And shadows of the night come hurtling on.

                    Edmonton
                    1977.02.02

London

The London I love is a quiet Sunday morning,
A walk on the heath with its wide rolling views,
The church and the village at Hampstead, the gardens,
The railings, the casements, the windows, the mews.

The London I love is the Regency Buildings,
The terraces, sweeping so grandly, abound;
The squares and the parks with magnificent mansions,
The streets where the cobblestones pattern the ground.

A stroll across Waterloo bridge in the sunshine,
The curve of the river, all dappled and blue,
The skyline beyond with ten thousand chimneytops,
Steeples and towers in a bright patchwork hue.

Photo: Jim MacCallum

The barges and tugs as they battle up river,
The pubs on the banks with heraldic designs
On the lintels and welcoming windows and doorways;
The thrill as a church tower distantly chimes.

The Tower and the Watergate, steeped in tradition,
The climb up the stairs of The Monument, grand,
Then hand-in-hand through picture-clad galleries,
An Albert Hall concert, a show at The Strand.

London is springtime with ducks on the Serpentine,
A boat on the water, a supper for two.
London is loneliness, sometimes and laughter,
London is memories for me - and for you.

Vancouver
1976.12.16

A Jambalaya Song

Feel the heat of the beat from the band-o!
Feel the throb from the pulse in my hand-o!
I'm sure that you now understand-o
That we're both very near Wonderland-o!

I can feel as we wheel in the sky-o
That we're both flying way oh-so-high-o,
But you must let me loosen my tie-o
- It feels grand with my hand on your thigh-o!

Atlanta to L.A.
1976.10.13

The next poem was started many years earlier. I never met anyone who matched it until I danced with a girl at Earl's Place in Atlanta. She inspired the last two verses - to the tune "I had to leave a little girl in Kingston Town".

Susan

I met a girl with eyes so brown
And her skin was golden - she was wondrous fair;
Her teeth were pearly and her lips were red
And the breezes made a melody of her hair.

And in the lamplight's subtle glow,
I can see her warm, deep and gentle gaze
From eyes set widely, and velvet cheeks,
And feel the rhythm of the dance in a loving daze.

Then as Time just glides away
And the evening changes to a hazy dream,
I see those red lips, brown eyes there,
But the maiden is as though she had never been!

Atlanta
1976.10.13

✽❤✽

Bilateral Nerve-type High-tone Deafness

I strolled along that garden path
Where autumn roses bloomed so fair
And saw the ripples on the pool,
There dancing in the autumn air.

The morning sky was azure blue
With silver moon just nearly faded,
And tiny wind-brushed clouds around
With golden edges faintly shaded.

A tree was there beside the way,
Its light-green leaves all shining lightly
And on each twig a tiny bird
- A thousand birds, all twittering brightly!

I thought, just then - it's been so long
Since last I heard their morning song!

Atlanta
1976.10.13

✳❤✳

The Last Flight from Prince George

Intermittent music breaking through the murmur
Of many sleepy people waiting for a 'plane -
Scuffling, shuffling footsteps,
                    talking, whispers, muttering
And many other noises just too complex to explain.

The sudden crazy whistle of the arms-detector stuttering
As it finds a pack of cigarettes and rates a nervous look
From people sitting nearest who were staring at the wall,
Or others sitting quietly and skipping through a book.

A little wave of expectation races through the hall,
Mothers, children, wheelchair-driven,
                    leave the growing throng
And head towards the orange aircraft standing in the rain
While some who're left move towards the door,
                    pretending nothing's wrong.

And then the mass departure to Vancouver, not the moon,
Leaves the hallway echoing that thin, recorded tune.

                    Vancouver
                    1976.09.02

Mairi in Glasgow
(Tune: "Den första gång jag såg dig")

You came with me to Dalsholm
On many a summer day.
The sky was hazy blue beyond the hill,
And down there in the valley,
The gasworks, tiny, lay
And Anniesland was peaceful, green and still.
We lay and watched the tracery
Of dappled treetops swaying;
We lay and heard the happy sound
Of distant children playing.
It was a lovely summer,
The days were long and bright,
And bright and blue your eyes were fondly shining.

✳❤✳

You walked with me by Kelvin
On many autumn eves.
The river murmured darkly, there below.
The muted sounds of twilight
Came filt'ring through the leaves,
Our lovers' steps were silent, measured, slow.
You held your arm around my waist,
Mine round your shoulders lying,
My every breath matched yours and matched
The evening breeze a-sighing.
The warmth of daytime sunshine
Rose gently all around
And added warmth to warmth between us burning.

You stood with me and whispered
The things that lovers say;
Our bodies trembled, young, excited, near.
The tramcar's passing flicker
Turned darkness into day,
We huddled close, pretending sudden fear.
The gaslight mantle guttered there
Its wan light vainly trying
To reach the darkest shadows where
We stood, our spirits flying.
Your eyes held such a promise
And glowed so deeply blue
And wove a spell, Eternity entwining.

Vancouver
1976.08.03

✳❤✳

Mum's Birthday Card

I'll bet you thought it was rotten
That your little boy had forgotten
That the twenty-third* of May
Was your very special day,
And that the great forgetful nit
Had once again forgotten it!

But no! Wee Colin saved the day
And sent the blooming card away.
But alas, your little honey
Just forgot to send some money!

Vancouver
1976.05.20

* In fact, I could never remember whether Mum's birthday was the 22nd
   or 23rd of May. It was the 22nd - so I ended up a day late this time
   anyway!

Elisabeth in the Morning

It's bright, and still, and the air from the window is cool.
The sun is up, and I think the birds are singing.
Your face is pink, and your lips are red and full
With the trace of a smile at a thought in a dream a-winging.

Your brow is smooth, and your hair is swept around
Your throat is pale and the pulse is soft as rain.
Your eyelids dance, at even the slightest sound,
And then relax, as the quietness comes again.

Your arms are round, and the wrists are slim and fine.
Your hands are strong and a little red with care.
My thoughts of the night are warm and rich as wine,
As I watch you, want you, love you, lying there.

It's hard to describe in words, at the time, how I feel,
But I never forget, and the feeling is beautifully real.

Vancouver
1976.04.07

✳❤✳

Lucky Old Mother

Mother is a lucky lass
- she insists, with rapture!
Last time she had a lucky break
- it was a compound fracture!

Vancouver
1976.04

Nancy Dowd Leaving Sandwell

Tripping barefoot down the aisle,
With your Monday morning smile,
Hair a-blow and hips a-swinging,
Sometimes whistling, sometimes singing,
You cheered us up - and tickled our fancy
- Good luck to you, Nancy!

Vancouver
1976.

Dave Pearson Leaving Sandwell

They'll miss you at Port Alice, Dave,
Smiling beard and all;
We'll miss you at Alberni too
- Good luck, then - from us all!

Vancouver
1976.06.30

Finlands besöket - på flyget hem

Ett sådant djävla längtande
Efter år av väntande
På nattens heta älskande
Med de vackra finska jäntarna.

Det krälar så av brudarna
Som jagar inn från skogarna
I Tamperes trånga krogarna
- man sprickar, ju, i fogarna!

Att kunna, då, med händarna
Smeka vita ländarna
Som hör till söta frändarna,
Det glider nu ur händarna.

Bortom allt beskrivande
Är detta djävla rivande!

Helsinki-Vancouver
1976-03.13

The Air Hostess

Outside is all dark, but the cabin is bright
And the aeroplane bustles with sounds of the flight
　　- CP 26 to Vancouver.
It's now very normal, familiar, to us
As when we once travelled on top of a bus,
　　Sensing the slightest manoeuvre.

And then, suddenly -

A dream of a girl in blue and green,
Hair in a swirl with a midnight sheen
And an eye both bright and smiling.
Our paths just touch in a moment of time,
Like swallows en route to a sunnier clime
　　And leave but a mem'ry, beguiling.

Prince George - Vancouver
1975.12.09

✳❤✳

90 Hyndland Street, Glasgow

It seems a waste of time to dream
        of twenty years ago,
But kaleidoscopic pictures simply come
        and then they go;
Patterns form and patterns fracture -
        sudden as a storm,
But the memory of the pictures
        keeps a body fine and warm.

We all have our childhood
        that the future cannot change -
The merry sparks a-dancing
        in the sullen kitchen range -
The welcome, warming kitchen
        and the cold out in the hall -
The clock upon the mantelpiece,
        The paintings on the wall.

"Is Colin coming out to play?" -
        the question at the door -
There's someone there I know so well -
        I've heard it all before -
And, sure enough, outside the glass
        I see a girlish form -
Yes - the memory of the pictures
        keeps a body fine and warm!

                West Vancouver
                1975.08.26

✼♥✼

Pamela Mansell

A face in the sunshine, all aglow -
The face of a girl I used to know -
Rounded brow and ruby lips -
Hazel eyes with pupils like black apple pips -
A yellow print dress with some sort of flowers,
Background all hazy, like mist after showers -
Smiling a smile that I once knew so well
- And a voice, in memory, rich as a bell.

A tiny wee scar on the cheek and the chin -
I made you fall in the race we were in.

What age are you now, at this instant, I wonder?
At the question, the picture starts crumbling asunder
- The smile fades, the eyes dim, her tears start to flow
- The dream was of twenty-three short years ago.

West Vancouver
1975.08.26

Chilean Dream Girl

Your eyes were closed, and, kissing hard
            with concentration's fire
The sweetness of the kisses
            was beyond a man's desire.
It's hard for me to understand and harder to explain
Why tears came flooding when I left
            to catch the waiting plane.
But, in that golden instant
            in the long expanse of time,
I would have lingered, quivering, eternity sublime.

Now, bruised and burning lips augment
            the memories left behind
Of hot and honeyed kisses
            just dissolving in my mind.

West Vancouver
1975.

GESA's Function*

GESA's function
At this junction
Is to spread the news
Of students, glad (?),
Designers, mad (?),
In kilt, or breeks, or trews.

Around this earth
There is no dearth
Of Babcock engineers
Who've been, by heck,
To Paisley Tech
And smutted Paisley beers.

They're scattered wide
From Causeyside
And far from all their peers.
So, in the main,
We help maintain
Contact through the years.

So, if you've time,
Then drop a line
To this, our own newsletter -
And, in a wink,
At least <u>you'll</u> think
It's suddenly got much better!

West Vancouver
1975.06.20

* - Babcock & Wilcox Ltd. Graduates and Students' Association

Thinking

I love to think in the kitchen sink
With my head tucked under my knee,
For I love the feel of a greasy heel
With a texture smooth as a jellied eel,
On my stubbled chin, you see.

I like to ponder, sitting yonder
In my favourite yoga-like stance,
Of girls with a yen for ugly wee men,
Rather than thrills with a fountain pen
Which could leak, just by mischance!

I can stare, just sitting there,
With my toes entwined round the chain,
At a passing car or a falling star,
While sucking a half-chewed candy bar
And dribbling down the drain.

It passes the time, to sit here and rhyme -
A defence mechanism, by heck,
Though the wife may scold and my feet grow cold
And the poem I write may never get sold,
It relieves the crick in my neck!

West Vancouver
1975.05.13

Presentation to Adelia Livesey
after Several Weeks of her Technical Writing Course with Sandwell

Pronouns, verbs, subordination,
With their awful fascination,
Rained on us like April showers.
But I think we did enjoy it,
And perhaps we'll all employ it -
So please accept these friendly flowers!

West Vancouver
1975.05.13

❤

Assignment for a Technical Writing Course

> I shouldn't have done it, I know,
> But the subjects were slower than slow.
> So I sat for an hour
> And here you've a shower
> Of lim'ricks* to give you a glow!
>
> That's all I've got for "the noo",
> But I can't resist writing for you!
> I hope you won't criticise,
> Blandish or witticise,
> Or take too stand-offish a view!

> West Vancouver
> 1975.05.05

* Please see the limericks at the end of this book.
The particular verses are in there somewhere!

Bröllopsdagen

> Ljusblå himmel, gröna ängar;
> Stilla sovrum, mjuka sängar;
> Mörka tider, lite gnäll
> (Man är inte alltid snäll).
> Tio ganska korta år -
> Äktenskapets ljuva vår.

> West Vancouver
> 1975.02.20

In English, translated 24 February 1996:

> Light-blue sky and greeny meadows,
> Quiet bedrooms, comfy bed-ohs;
> Troubled moments, little grumble
> (You see, one isn't always humble).
> Ten years, short as any-thing -
> This is wedlock's lovely Spring.

❤

The Architect and the Engineer

The Engineer and the Architect
Disagree one day
As to who should design a railway line
From here to the Milky Way.

Says the Engineer, a mite austere,
"It's obvious to me,
That your background is too profound
To design it usefully.

You'd take your pen, and I know you'd then
Never think of the cost
And then I'd find it one hell of a grind
Getting your lines uncrossed!"

The Architect is most disturbed
At the tone of the Engineer,
Which confirms what he knew of the Engineer crew
- But that isn't much, I fear!

He replies, with his eyes on the pies in the skies
"Some of that may be true;
But the main design of this railway line
Will have to be beautiful too!

The first long run, from Earth past the sun -
I don't care what you think -
Will mainly consist of a helical twist
In a delicate, lustrous, pink."

The Engineer winced, completely convinced,
As he tugged at his navy-blue collar,
That the Architect's dream was all peaches and cream
And that he had forgotten the dollar!

I'm trying to say, in my devious way,
That a scion of either profession,
Will not understand what the other has planned,
But you'll never obtain that confession!

Vancouver
1975.04.08

❤

Househunting

Elisabeth, quite full of glee,
Hunts a house with passion!
But when she gets to number three
I hope she's had her ration!

Gothenburg
1974.03.24

Aunt Nancy's Visit to Calderpark Zoo

Our Aunt got locked in at the zoo!
I wonder - could that be true?
It must have been fun
Just sucking her thumb
And turning a pale shade of blue!

The tigers liked having her there,
Enthroned on a lavatory chair;
"If she gets much thinner
then we'll get no dinner!"
Said a specially ravenous pair.

She shouted all night it is said,
Till her face turned a deep rosy red.
Said one lion to another
"I think that's your mother -
should she not be at home in her bed?"

When day broke they found her, awake,
And soothingly offered her cake.
She'll *be* back again
Come wind, hail, or rain,
But she'll never repeat that mistake!

Gothenburg
1970.12.21

❤

Adam och Marie

Att dikta på svenska är inte så lätt -
En kille kan slutligen tappa sitt vett!
Vad tjänar det också att kämpa och slita
Med mässing och brons, färg eller krita?
Men livet har glada och ljuvliga stunder
När man tror man kan samtliga evighets grunder;
Men trots minnet mörknar, jag tror jag ska' minnas
Att snygga konstnärliga tjejer än finnes!

Uppsala?, 1970.12.01

In English, translated 25 February 1996:

Rhyming in Swedish is not just a cinch
A fellow could loose all his wits in a pinch!
What do you gain then by fighting and straining
With brass and with bronze, painting and crayoning?
But life has delicious and lighthearted phases
When you think you know all of Eternity's bases;
I think I'll recall, though my memory's unsound
That pretty and arty young maids are still found!

Elisabeth's Thirtyfirst Birthday

A pot for your birthday shows lack of romance,
Like a tie for a husband or fella,
But the candles I hope, help to brighten it up
With their red, blue, and orangey yella!

They'll last many hours, and I'm sure we'll have fun
And share many "mysiga kvällar"   (pleasant evenings)
O'er a nice cosy meal, with a glass of good wine,
By the light of the red, blue and yella!

Gothenburg, 1970.10.05

❤

Averill's Red Kockum Pot

If you don't like cooking with pots that are red -
You can aye shove the thing under the bed!

Gothenburg
1969.06.27

Nu ska' vi borsta dina tänder

Nu ska' vi borsta dina tänder,
  Vita berg på munnens stränder.
Du får hålla pappas händer
- Öppna munnen nu!

Gothenburg, 1969.

In English, translated 25 February 1996:

We're going to brush your teeth just now
Tiny mountains white as snow
You can hold Dad's hand and show
        them
- Open widely *now*!

To Aunt Nancy -
On a Crash Diet in the Western Infirmary, Glasgow

Poor old you - lying there,
Can't even munch a piece of pear
Or chew upon a bit of apple
- Just water now to wet your thrapple!

Meringues and cream cakes, coffee too,
Are all, I'm sure, taboo for you.

The only consolation now
To smooth the furrows on your brow
As you think on that Sunday rasher
- You'll come out a seven-stone smasher!

Gothenburg, 1967.07.18

✳❤✳

To Bert Smith -
A 45-year-old Is Congratulated at Cactus-time 1967

A card with a cactus should not be obscure
And more to the point than this beauty, I'm sure;
Its message of cheer isn't hard to derive -
It's many more years till you reach 85.

Gothenburg
1967.01.06

Bert never reached 85 - he died in a car smash in 1986.

Elisabeth

We were a boy and a girl on a rock by the river,
Tumbling and roaring and rushing away,
Watching the swoop of the wave-daring swallows
And our hearts came together - as hearts sometimes may.

Your eyes had the sparkle of blue open water,
Dappled in sunlight and tossed into spray,
Warm and caressing as waves on the shingle
In a rich creaming necklace encircling the bay.

It seems such an age since we roamed through the woodland
To the place where the wild rosy strawberries lay,
While the bees filled the air with their summery murmur
And the birdsong was still, in the heat of the day.

How warmly the teardrops came falling, my darling,
As your words touched my heart in a fathomless way,
Drawing us close on the path of a lifetime,
Where by chance we have met - and perchance we shall stay.

London
1964.09.01

E.I.O.

He was a Glasgow keelie wi' the ginger o' his race,
Bonny blue eyes and a kind wee face;
He wasnae verra fast, but then, you couldnae ca' him slow
- It took him forty winks tae steal my E.I.O.

When I was wee I dandled on my mother's homely knee,
She told me o' the folk I'd meet and o' the things I'd see,
It was nice o' her tae warn me, but how was she tae know
I wouldnae much mind partin' wi' my E.I.O.

When I grew up tae womanhood, both tall and fair and slim,
I met a fella by the gate, and he seemed fu' o' vim;
That's the kind tae watch - I mind ma mammy telt me so
- All he's really after is yer E.I.O.!

He was a Glasgow keelie wi' the ginger o' his race,
Bonny blue eyes and a kind wee face;
He wasnae verra fast, but then, you couldnae ca' him slow
- It took him forty winks tae steal my E.I.O.

London
1964.06.26

✹❤✹

With an Unofficial Birthday Present

Vee -
You laugh like a child with a handful of daisies
Plucked from the lawn on a bright summer's day.
My troubles recede and those few precious moments
Become to me, quite unforgettably gay!

Your smile can be sad, with a faraway dreaming,
Or loving and warm as the spark in your eye,
As fresh and as bright as the sun in the morning,
Chasing the darkness and lighting the sky.

Serene as the moonlight on snow-covered mountains,
Calm as the loch in the lee of the hill,
Sure in your robes of the full bloom of womanhood
The mem'ries will linger and live with me still.

London
1964.05.23

❤ *Valentine 1964 (Deb)* ❤

A rhyme every time is as hard to maintain
As the nails on the lid of a coffin!
So, all I can say - I'm glad Valentine's Day
Doesn't come round much more often!

And now, don't be arch, on the seventh of March
I'm thinking of doing some skating,
So if you'd like to come, then write to me, chum,
And for Heaven's sake - don't keep me waiting!

London
1964.02

❈❤❈

❤ *Valentine's Day 1964 (Pat L.)* ❤

Since it's Valentine's Day, Pat,
I'll tell you - with some hesitation,
You've the sweetest brown eyes in Creation,
- and I must put you wise
That the stars in those eyes
Play havoc with <u>my</u> circulation!

See you later - Circulator!*

London
1964.02

* This lass worked in the Design Engineering Department with Babcock
in London, England, doing boiler circulation calculations
- most ably.

Reasons - For and Against!

Lying with you*, in the dark,
Warm as toast and honey sweet,
Wishing you would think of somewhere
Else to put your frozen feet!

Skin a-tingle, lips a-fire,
Feelings soaring ever higher,
Then you pinch my share of blanket,
      Cooling my desire!

Loving, in a rosy darkness,
Touching, cheek to knee,
Then you softly murmur - "Dolling -
It's <u>your</u> turn to make the tea!"

London
1964.01

* <u>Not</u> Pat L.

❤

Vera

A nurse I have met on my travels,
With ankles as neat as her dress,
Dispenses a hangover potion
Encouraging sweet drunkenness!

London
1963.08.16

Jilted - A Ring For Your Finger

I've a ring for your finger with a sapphire of blue,
Engraved, oh, so neatly, from me just for you,
Though the words there are written so permanently
There's only a wish where your finger should be.

There are diamonds that sparkle like droplets of rain
That fall on the machar and nourish the grain,
But all of the raindrops that fall in the sea
Could ne'er fill the hole where your finger should be.

Though the pine tree can grow on a rocky hill side
And the marram grass flourish though lapped by the tide,
The red rowan berry would grow to a tree
If only your finger were where it should be.

Though autumn must come and the berries must fall
And the scythe of The Reaper is sharpened for all,
You'll stay young and lovely and my memory
Will aye fill the place where your finger should be.

CMacC to DEB
London
1963.08.16

Marchin' Wi' the H.L.I. [*]

I cam' up fae Anderston tae jine the H.L.I.,
When I went hame in the uniform, my lassie said "My, my,

> Ye're a dandy Jock, a handy Jock,
> Marchin' wi' the H.L.I.!"

I went tae see the RSM and the Adjutant as well
And they pit me in "C" Company tae train there for a spell.

> Ye're a dandy Jock, ...

It disnae matter which platoon, they're smashers every one,
As they stride along, they sing this song
> and they sparkle in the sun.

> Ye're a dandy Jock, ...

Although the Fusiliers are smart, the Argylls and Seaforths too,
They're no a patch on the H.L.I. and the lassies ken that too!

> Ye're a dandy Jock, a handy Jock,
> Marchin' wi' the H.L.I.!

> London
> 1963.07.25

* 5th/6th Battalion, Highland Light Infantry (Territorial Army)

❤

Hot-line Jingle

Calling you, dear, on the telephone, sets me in a whirl.
It's not every day, 'cause it's a long, long way
        To my long distance girl.

Chorus: Life is swingin' when the phone bell's ringin'
       And I forget I'm feelin' so blue!
       My heart is dancin' when we're telephone romancin'
          Does your heart go ting-a-ling too?

Drop in the pennies one by one, pennies by the score;
It's the next best thing to having you near
        A-knocking on my door!

I feel so happy when the phone bell rings, shrilling jauntily
But the thrill I want is the thrill I'll get
        When you're engaged to me!

My money all goes on ringing you - a ransom for a queen -
Let's forget the cost and get our lines crossed
        - Our marriage lines I mean!

               London
               1963.05.17

❤

My Sunshine

There's a bright star on my horizon
And it points the way to you;
It's gleaming brightly on my horizon,
Calling me to you.

You were mine, dear, for just a moment,
A fleeting instant, all sublime,
You have flown, love, my golden prize gone,
Leaving me with wintertime.

The wind goes rustling through the treetops
And it whispers as it goes
That I miss you, dear, I love you,
My sweet and longed for summer rose.

It's ever sunset on my horizon
When you're far across the darkening sea,
But there'll be sunrise on my horizon
When you bring sunshine home to me.

Glasgow
1963.04

�֍❤֍

❤ *Longing, Longing, Longing* ❤
(Valentine's Day 1963)

Rhyming isn't easy
 when you're far across the seas,
Black and cold and creamed with foam
 from winter's icy breeze.
Half my heart's in Norway, Deb,
 watching over you,
The other piece is here with me
 and wishing it were too!

My nights are long with yearning
 and the days slip slowly by;
I long to walk and laugh with you
 beneath the summer sky.
Though every hill's a mountain
 and every inch a mile,
I'll get by with mem'ries
 and your picture for a while.

The long June days are calling,
 they're not so far away,
Then there's an end to loneliness
 and skies of sombre grey;
I'll love you then as I love you now,
 for longer, pet, by far,
Than the time it takes to walk from here
 to the twinkling evening star.

No words can ever tell you
 just how much you mean to me,
So I hope you'll be my Valentine
 for nineteen sixty-three.

Glasgow
1963.01.20

❄❤❄

Lines from a Catch Phrase I've Heard Somewhere!

When concrete ideas keep dissolving
- And your mind is in circles revolving -
Then count up to three, and come and see me
And you'll find things all quickly resolving!

SNAP!

And they did!

Whoopee!

Glasgow
1962.11.27

Well - Why Then?

If I had been born a thousand years hence,
Or even a hundred years ago,
We could never have met in the summer time,
Or walked through woods and meadows.

If you had been born on some other star
Even though the time were the same,
We could never have shared the happiness
Of just being alive together.

Can you tell me why we happen to be
In the same little valley of Time?
Can is be Chance, or is it Design
That draws us close in the sunlight?

So, Deb, let your doubts and worries fade
And cleave to me for ever,
And we will travel the lifelong way,
Hand in hand to the rainbow's end.

London
1962.08.20

✳❤✳

Skit on Serena's Engagement
(Tune: The Rose of Tralee)

The pale moon was raaaiiising above the old churchyard
When word came to me that Serena was lost,
Noo I'm tearin' my hair oot in muckle great handfu's
'Tis the first time I ever, in love, have been crossed!

Chorus:
She was luvlee and fair as the roses in the summer,
But it was not her beauty alone that won me;
Oh no, 'twas the light in the eyes ever shining
O' the wee siller coo on her ain manteltree.

Oh call out the valleys, the glens and the shipyards,
Take up the claymore and come follow me!
We'll drive all the Tories and stinkin' rich fermers
Wi' whackin' great subsidies into the sea!

Glasgow
1962.06.08

♥

Christmas Eve in Aviemore

When the moon is high in the winter sky
And the air is keen and clear -
When the hills have a white and silvery light
And seem so wondrous near -
When the sparks blow higher from the Yule log fire
And the songs are sweet and merry -
With room and hall decked overall
With cards and holly berry -
Then I think of you, in palest yellow,
Rich dark hair and hazel eyes
Glowing deep and mellow.

I hear your voice, like a heather bell
On a quiet hill, in a pink sunrise,
Casting a 'witching spell.

PS:
If you think this verse is somewhat terse
- Oh - I never praised your nose -
If you think this is bad, then you better 'ad
Not read my gems of prose!

London
1962.01.21

❊❤❊

❤ *From a Dither, In a Dither, To a Dither, Deb* ❤
(Valentine's Day 1962)

When you dilly-dally and you won't make up your mind,
When you swither and you dither to and fro;
When you shilly-shally like a leaflet in the wind,
You are quite the most annoying girl I know!

Since last July you've kept me in the strangest sort of muddle,
The way those silly notions come and go;
Why must we always chatter
 when you know I want a cuddle
From you, the most exciting girl I know?

Your eyes, your smile, your silky cheek,
your hair, surpassing fine,
Have won the battle quite some time ago,
So please decide this once
 and say you'll be my Valentine,
'Cos you're certainly the nicest girl I know!

London
1962.01.18

✳❤✳

Memories of Mairi

I never imagined, two years ago today,
I'd know you so well or so long,
And now the story's finished
 I'm sending you this card
With a memory to tide us both along.

Murrayfield - a shooting star,
The castle, bright as day,
That meeting in the rifle range
 seems no time away.
Hueval in the sunshine -
Tangasdale in the rain,
A blue-eyed girl, her hair all curls,
On the pier at Castlebay.

Kelvingrove just after dark,
Parties at the Corps -
Just some of the memories
- There's half a million more.

Glasgow
1961.02.14

A'Mhairi

Eyes in the lamplight, glowing like fire,
Eyes in the sunshine, clear as sapphire,
Eyes in the twilight that comes before sleep,
Eyes I will always, in memory, keep.

Infinite depth in the blue of her eyes,
Reaching much deeper than clear summer skies,
Depths as profound as the deepest blue sea
Shall remain in the depths of my memory.

Glasgow
1959.10

❤

Paddy

She's with me every dreaming moment,
Walks with me 'neath cloudless skies,
Makes me happy, smile with gladness
With each warm glance from her gray-green eyes.

The birds sing louder, longer, sweeter,
The grass, the trees are greener still,
The lochans bluer, stars are brighter
And each old sight is a brand-new thrill.

She holds my hand and makes me tingle
As she used to, Yesterday,
Then I awake, the castles crumble,
And joy and gladness flee away.

Glasgow
1959.09.06

❤ *Mairi* ❤
(Valentine's Day 1959)

Her eyes are as blue as the islands' skies
In the calm of a summer's day;
Her hair is as dark as the raven's wing
In the trees above the bay;
Her voice has the music of the long green waves
And I'd love to hear her say
That she'd be mine for a little time,
Mine on Saint Valentine's Day.

Glasgow
1959.02.12

❤

Patricia

She, who lies with her hair
 a tumbled golden sea on the pillow,
 her cheek warmly velvet 'gainst mine;
She, whose eyes are green as the coverlet,
 glowing with love,
 promising much, withholding nothing;
She, her breath gentle and sweet,
 through lips slightly parted,
 lips soft and warm as the fire in my heart,
         Is my Patricia.

                Glasgow
                1956

Babcock Lassies

Connie

Hair a brown wave on shoulders of cream,
Tall and sleek, with the coolest of eyes,
Eyes blue, flecked with gold, toned with surprise
Or a faraway look as in mind of a dream.

                ?

     Wide blue eyes and raven hair,
     Ankles neat in bright red shoes,
     Turquoise coat, swinging free
     And a come-hither look in her eyes for me
     - And you - and you - and you!

                ?

Her carriage is dreadful and she wears glasses too,
But her fair hair's neat and tidy
And I like her eyes of blue.
I've never spoken to her, I'd like to, mind you,
I'm sure she'll have a lovely voice
To match those eyes of blue.

                Glasgow
                1956.10

✳❤✳

An Anniversary Poem

Though the years go by and our frames grow old
Our hearts will be young as the spring -
We will still be in love, as in days of old
When the blood in our veins was as molten gold,
Though life's autumn has ousted the spring.

Two years have gone by since that warm August eve
When love's arrow sank deep in our hearts,
There to lodge for the span of our lives, I believe
And beyond, so making it pointless to grieve
O'er our youth which will one day depart.

I know I will love you, though I'm old and grey,
With a love just as true as it was at the first
And my eyes will e'er see you as young as that day,
Still as vital, alive, exciting and gay
As you were then, so love and adore you I must.

> Ayios Nikolaos, Cyprus
> 1955.08.13

Small Comfort

Cracked columns of marble against the blue,
Broken tiles barely showing through windblown sand,
Weatherworn statues with features long gone,
    Are of the past.

Buildings of concrete in grey smoky skies,
Floors brightly gleaming with plastic designs,
Conceptions in wire, without meaning to most,
    Are of the present.

The future is hazy, uncertain as aye,
But dawning and sunsets, the hills and the sea,
Will go on forever, though my friends and I,
    Are of the past.

> Ayios Nikolaos, Cyprus
> 1955.08

Unending Strife

The golden Day flees over the hills to the west
From the Evening, who then rules the earth for a space
'Til his brother, the evening mist, climbs to the throne,
Subduing the world with his feathery mace.
He is but courageous while Light is his friend;
When he fades and then dies, his craven heart quails
As Darkness draws nigh in his harness of stars,
Conquering silently, mountains and dales
Unopposed. The Mist, treacherous one that he is,
Surrenders to Darkness, who grants him his life;
So he serves in Night's armies, but dies when the Sun
Stabs to his heart with his first glancing knife
Of sunlight, his life's blood falling as dew,
Imparting new strength to Dawn, feeble and grey.

Night foresees his defeat and flies from the Light,
A phoenix, reborn in the fire of new Day.

                            Ismailia
                            1955.05

❤ *Valentine Rhymes - Especially for Typists* ❤

> You never hear St Valentine's
> Secretary griping
> I understand that she prefers
> The touching to the typing!

———

> For typists who are ambidextrous,
> Pregnancy is most infectious!
> Look around! Happy Valentine's!

———

✳❤✳

Here we are at Valentine's
No fun to be away -
But be patient and you'll get
A kiss another day!

―――――

If male sexuality's
A problem for you all
Then take comfort, for you'll find
- It's better than none at all!

―――――

You'll get no private rhymes this year -
I don't want sued
From here .... to here!

―――――

Old-fashioned typists are divine
For they can be your Valentine.
New type machines are not for me
- They're not much fun upon your knee!

―――――

Circular:
Upside down or round about,
Love's as sweet as wine;
So, in this topsy-turvy world,
Please be my Valentine!

―――――

The message on this card was written
By a fussy man -
But I like to be kissed or bitten -
Anytime you can!

❃❤❃

LIMERICKS

A limerick puts into rhyme
A transient thought at a time
When one lies there and ponders
Or when one's mind wanders
To things rather less than sublime.

Country Compromise

Compromise, make no mistake,
Cuts the town trips that you make,
So the lady who led
Her two sows to get bred
Could surely have given them cake?

To Ted Walker and For All Retired TypeS

A shadow was cast by Ted's Pome
On old guys who presently roam
- You're not silly old farts -
- Make a play for those tarts,
Before Age's arrow strikes home!

Before you go'n' do yourself harm,
Here's a thought that should still keep you warm
- Many comely young tarts
Love their silly old farts
For their money, if not for their charm!

Hornby Island Sea-lions

That sea-lion sipping her tea
Drew a wonderful picture for me.
  There's only one thing -
  Does she sit there and sing
And balance her cup on her knee?

Or maybe she sits on the beach
With her sugar and milk and a peach,
  While she stares at the moon
  And uses her spoon
To scratch all the bits she can't reach.

Or maybe that sea-lion's a male
With a much more remarkable tail
  Which he waves as a fan
  Like an uncultured man
To cool down his tea in a pail.

And though I just can't stand the stuff,
I envision them both taking snuff
  When they finish their tea
  On that rock by the sea,
Be it limpid, or wavy and rough.

The sea-lions on Hornby are rare,
So if you see this elegant pair,
  Don't scare them away,
  We'd like them to stay
And come to the Annual Fair!

                    Hornby Island
                    1993.10.31

❤

Critical Political

It crosses my personal grain
To bring to my fellow man, pain,
    So, to each politician
    I'd assign a mortician
And a large overdose of cocaine.

―――

In ten years our money has halved
Through someone's political craft.
    Did Mr Mulrooney,
    Who gave us the "loonie",
Surreptitiously give us the shaft?

―――

Bouchard treats Quebec as his loot.
'Tis "Treason" he plays on his lute.
    In earlier times
    He would hang for his crimes
- I'd string him up by his foot!!

―――

Bouchard's clear agenda - his own -
Behind every whine and each groan,
    If he has his way
    He'll rule, one fine day,
On Quebec's new imperial throne.!

―――

In spite of each PQ demand,
Though they bite the Canadian hand,
    We're all better by far
    If we stay as we are
With Quebec as a part of this land.

�֍❤֍

———

MP's pension critique is sedition.
They ignore each appealing petition.
  Despite pious noise
  All of Chrétien's boys
Maintain the pork-barrel tradition.

———

Trudeau, who some love and some shun,
Had a splendid political run;
  Not just attractive
  And publicly active,
- Had a daughter at seventy-one!

———

With pronouncements courageous and weighty,
From Quebec to the trouble in Haiti,
  Trudeau's application
  Inspires admiration
- Perhaps he'll have twins when he's eighty!

———

Canadians see it balloon
The deficit's nearing the moon
  Preston Manning's the man
  With a definite plan
To cut out the deficit soon!

———

We'd all have much cause to rejoice
If Preston could spruce up his voice;
  That Calgary (?) drawl
  Tends to irritate all
And makes both my armpits quite moist.

✳❤✳

A keen market gardener from Leeds
Once swallowed a packet of seeds
    And the packet as well.
    He landed in Hell,
As the Chief Cultivator of Weeds!

———

I slept in a bedroom in Ealing
With a lady tattooed on the ceiling.
    She had lovely blue eyes
    And muscular thighs
And she gave me a curious feeling.

———

A snail finds the secret of travel
Exceedingly hard to unravel.
    He does it all wrong
    As he slithers along,
And scrapes his wee arse* on the gravel!

———

* If you are a bit of a prude,
  and find such words 'specially rude,
    For "arse" read "behind",
    if it preys on your mind
- I hope that this lightens your mood!

———

A cheeky young chappie called Chalmers
Wore red-, green-, and gold-striped pyjamas.
    His girlfriends all said,
    As he leapt into bed,
"Take them off, Charles -
    you know they alarm us!"

———

✳❤✳

A portly young maiden called Nellie
Had a very protuberant belly.
   It got used, in a jam,
   As a battering ram,
Or a shelf for a portable telly!

———

A lad from East Cheam, of all places,
Had a wife who had no social graces
   She'd jump into bed
   At a nod of his head,
Or a movement to loosen his braces!

———

A man had a passionate wife
With a habit that often caused strife
   She'd swing on his ear
   By her teeth and I fear
That he oftentimes feared for his life!

———

A shy maiden lady called Ruth
(I swear that I'm telling the truth!)
   When the full moon is clear,
   If you look at her ear,
There's the mark of a passionate tooth!

———

A musician who lived in The Hague
Contracted a curious ague -
   He coughed in adagio
   And sneezed in arpeggios.
Thy diagnosed harmonic plague!

———

✳❤✳

A laddie in downtown Toronto,
Was uncertain which bus to get on to.
　　He dithered around,
Took the wrong underground,
Now nobody knows where he's gone to!

———

In the year two thousand and one,
A spacecraft flew too near the sun.
　　It encountered a flare
　　And was vapourized there
- For the crewmen it wasn't much fun.

———

A gourmet who liked rhyming slang,
Had a sausage go off with a bang;
　　The Scot said "I'm blowed,
　　I thought it was toad-
in-the-hole - and I find I was wrang".

———

A cranky old craven from Crail
Enjoyed a nice tender boiled snail.
　　So the things wouldn't harm her,
　　Wore a full suit of armour
- she feared they'd a sting in their tail!

———

I once met a girl on a 'plane
From America going to Spain.
　　She sat by the aisle,
　　With a very sweet smile
But her dialect gave me a pain!

———

❤

We all knew a lady from Luss
Who used to come visiting us.
    She was shopping one day,
    In her own dreamy way,
And went and walked under a bus!

———

There's a publican called Gassy Deighton
Whose friends think he's really a great one;
    He's a gen'rous old sod,
    But he eats like a hog,
And we've noticed he's putting the weight on!

———

While bathing off Dar-es-Salaam,
I got in a bit of a jam.
    I stepped off some rocks
    In bright yellow socks
And my left foot got caught in a clam!

Sinister - eh?

———

A pernickety old polar bear
Once got a terrible scare
    He ate an explorah
    Beneath the aurorah
And found he wore pink underwear.

———

On a branch sat a young turtledove,
Who felt he was falling in love
    He found he was wrong
    When he finished his song
And his lady friend gave him a shove!

———

❤

A forward young man from Le Moynt
Felt the maiden had quite missed the poynt -
 When he made a pass
 At the lass in the grass,
She pushed his nose right out of joynt!

———

Ted Walker

A persistent old poet called Ted
Writes his poetry lying in bed.
 He doesn't count sheep -
 He could write in his sleep,
Writing rhymes rattling round in his head.

If he goes to Heaven, I'm sure
It won't be because he is pure,
 But in difficult times
 Such nonsensical rhymes
Have a certain sublimal allure.

———

A soldier who lived in a trench
And was known to be good at his French
 When offered some cheese,
 Proclaimed to the breeze,
"Je ne peux pas manger - pour le stench"!

———

A girl from the centre of town
Longed to get lovely and brown.
 She sat in the sun
 From seven till one,
And got burnt to a cinder, the clown!

———

When Westinghouse put out their ad.
Young Wedgewood became hopping mad.
   "At Dounreay, in Britain,
   It's OUR atoms we're splittin'
On the cheap. So, keep off!" said the lad.

———

A rare old baboon at the zoo
Lived alone and had nothing to do.
   Till a visit, one Yule,
   To a well-known boy's school
Taught him to flagellate* too.

* The use of the word "flagellate"
  Has become rather common, of late.
   Such writers are those
   Whose sixpenny prose
Might make a monk masturbate.

———

A shark in a southern clime
Committed a real heinous crime -
   He found in the waters,
   Five men and their daughters
And then had a whale of a time!

———

A grip on a glunge with a gorge,
Little punk and his mate, nicknamed George,
   And a girlie called Fanny
   Took a kick at his granny
Then stood up and a-grinding a worge!*

   * Authentic dream line!

———

❈♥❈

INDEX OF FIRST LINES